G000124660

market
prophets

market prophets

Can forecasters predict the financial future?

DAVID STAMP

REUTERS

Published by **Pearson Education**

London ■ New York ■ Toronto ■ Sydney ■ Tokyo ■ Singapore ■ Hong Kong
Cape Town ■ New Delhi ■ Madrid ■ Paris ■ Amsterdam ■ Munich ■ Milan ■ Stockholm

PEARSON EDUCATION LIMITED

Head Office:
Edinburgh Gate
Harlow CM20 2JE
Tel: +44 (0)1279 623623
Fax: +44 (0)1279 431059

London Office:
128 Long Acre
London WC2E 9AN
Tel: +44 (0)20 7447 2000
Fax: +44 (0)20 7240 5771
Website: www.financialminds.com
         www.reuters.com

_____

First published in Great Britain in 2002

© David Stamp 2002

The right of David Stamp to be identified as Author
of this Work has been asserted by him in accordance
with the Copyright, Designs and Patents Act 1988.

ISBN 1 903 68407 2

British Library Cataloguing in Publication Data
A CIP catalogue record for this book can be obtained from the British Library

10 9 8 7 6 5 4 3 2 1

Typeset by Pantek Arts Ltd, Maidstone, Kent
Printed and bound in Great Britain by Biddles Ltd, Guildford and Kings Lynn

The Publishers' policy is to use paper manufactured from sustainable forests.

To Eva, Frances and Fiona, of course

contents

about the author

David Stamp was born in Newcastle upon Tyne in the northeast of England in 1958. After studying German at Liverpool University and journalism at University College, Cardiff, he joined Reuters in 1981 as a trainee reporter. Since then he has completed postings in Hong Kong, New Zealand, Austria, the Netherlands and the Czech Republic. He has reported from central and eastern Europe before and after the fall of Communism as well as from the former Yugoslavia, Australia and the South Pacific. Since 1997 he has worked for Reuters in London, focusing on forecasts for the British and continental European economies. David lives just outside the capital with his wife and two daughters. He is happiest away from the crowded southeast of England, walking on the hills of Northumberland.

preface

"Among all forms of mistake, prophecy is the most gratuitous."
– George Eliot, *Middlemarch*

Only at mid-career did I get to know the Market Prophets. I had spent many happy years touring the world as a reporter with Reuters, the international news organization. I had trudged the dismal streets of Bucharest and Sofia under two of Communism's more brutal regimes. I had covered Chris Patten, the last Governor of Hong Kong, slugging it out with China over the territory's political future. I had made reporting trips to Papua New Guinea and the ruins of Bosnia-Herzegovina. But after almost 15 years on the road I returned to London, my home base. It was then that I encountered the men and women who predict for a living.

The prediction business is immense. It stretches from fortune telling and futurism to weather forecasting and business planning. In my job at Reuters headquarters I encountered only one branch of what William Sherden, a debunker of most forms of forecasting, calls "the second oldest profession."[1] But this branch, which itself can be split into at least two divisions and many subdivisions, is big enough to employ many thousands of people around the world.

In London I joined the Reuters Polling Unit, a small part of a large news organization which embodies two elements of the modern economy: recycling and adding value. On the unit we collected forecasts, put them into an Excel spreadsheet, worked out the average expectation – known rightly or wrongly as the "consensus" – and wrote a news report about the results. The predictions themselves were varied: usually they had something to do with money. Where would the stock market stand at the end of the year? Was the economy heading for greater growth or recession next year? Would the European Central Bank change interest rates next week? When would the euro pull out of its nosedive and would Britain ever adopt it? Across the world from New York to Tokyo and Oslo to Johannesburg colleagues would likewise gather expectations on their patch. The formula was simple but popular. Polling is a participation sport. Analysts and economists who gave us their predictions seemed anxious to know what the others thought and how they stood compared with The Consensus. But why? How did they come up with the forecasts anyway? Are they ever right? Should we believe a word they say? As I got to know the Market Prophets better I began to ask myself these questions. Perhaps I should have done so sooner.

Here I should make clear what is probably obvious from my brief curriculum vitae: I am no Market Prophet myself. In researching this book I spoke not only to people who make the predictions but those who had to act upon them. One such was Ken Clarke. He ran Britain's finances as Chancellor of the Exchequer for four years with just one paper qualification that was relevant: an Advanced Level examination pass in economics taken as an 18-year-old schoolboy. That's one up on me. Clarke cheerfully noted that we both had to judge the pundits based on "my A level and your complete lack of any qualification in economics." Yet we both relied on forecasts in our daily life and could come a cropper if they proved to be wrong – and we had believed them.

Clarke had to worry about the economic well-being of a nation, plus his own political neck. I, by contrast, had to worry about only the financial well-being of me and my family. Even in this modest endeavor I found myself relying on the Market Prophets. As I prepared to write this book my wife "suggested" that we rebuild our ramshackle kitchen. That meant pushing up the mortgage but should we borrow on a fixed or a floating interest rate? In other words we had to bet on whether the Bank of England would raise or cut rates in the coming years. While abroad we saved some money which we hope one day will help our daughters through university. Should we leave it sitting in a savings account or take a punt on the stock market? We did buy some shares, naturally just as the market peaked. Should we bail out, or hold on in the hope that stocks will bounce back before our girls start heading to college in 2010? Should I buy some euros for next summer's holiday now, or wait till we go for a better exchange rate?

Like it or not most of us have to make these choices and we have only two options: rely on fate or rely on the Market Prophets. This book won't tell you how to forecast the euro or predict the Dow – there are plenty of self-help guides out there. It offers instead a glimpse of how the Market Prophets work and whether they succeed. It's written for people who may not even have an A level in economics, but need to know. Like me.

Note

1 *The Fortune Sellers*, by William A. Sherden, John Wiley and Sons, 1998.

acknowledgments

Our appetite for predictions has sucked ever more economists and stock analysts into punditry, some willingly, others less so. Forecasters are frequently the face that banks present to the media, and no doubt many people who appear in this book are under orders to win coverage for themselves and their companies. Some admit as much. But to brand them all as mere publicity-seekers – apart from the obvious exceptions revealed in the book – would be wrong. While I researched *Market Prophets* many people gave me help far beyond what was needed to get the literary equivalent of a sound bite. Yet few of them had much time to spare. Less than a fortnight after I began my work the suicide hijackers attacked America, claiming six Reuters colleagues among the thousands of victims. The weeks and months that followed were tough for anyone trying to predict the economic and financial consequences. I was also struck by how frankly economists, perhaps more so than stock analysts, discussed the frailties of their forecasts. No one who was simply out for cheap publicity would do that. Other people in this book were under no such orders but nevertheless still patiently explained their work to me.

In particular I should like to thank the following in the United States: Victor Zarnowitz for a frank assessment of economic forecasting born of more than 30 years' study; Alan Blinder for recalling his times, some bruising, at the Federal Reserve; Bruce Kasman and David Greenlaw for dissecting Fed watching; Peter Bernstein for a ready supply of evidence, anecdotal and academic, on the record of forecasters; Prakash Loungani for explaining his own research and pointing me to other work in the field; and Alan Shaw for an entertaining explanation of the rivalry between chartists and fundamentalists.

In Britain I'm most grateful to Charlie Bean for an exhaustive explanation of his thoughts on forecasting, although he was wrestling with the consequences of September 11 at the time; Ken Clarke, who was amusing as ever in relating the tensions between forecasters and policymakers; Charles Goodhart for an impromptu tutorial at the London School of Economics; Dave Jubb and Harry Smith for steering me through the mysteries of artificial intelligence; and Danny Gabay for contrasting forecasting in central banking and the financial markets. Many others in London, Edinburgh, Frankfurt, Zurich and Tokyo also helped me greatly including Klaus Baader, Roy Batchelor, Tony Dye, Marc Faber, Richard Jeffrey, Naka Matsuzawa, Andrew Milligan, Adolf Rosenstock, Michael Schubert, Kirit Shah, Hiromichi Shirakawa, Ken Wattret, and Trevor Williams.

I'm also indebted to Peter Osler for both explaining his work as an economist and correcting parts of my manuscript and making suggestions. At Reuters a number of colleagues helped me in many ways. They include Nigel Stephenson, Hament Bulsara, Svea Herbst-Bayliss, Shin Kishima, Christina Fincher and Janet Guttsman.

MetaStock charts are provided courtesy of Equis International, a Reuters group company.

Thanks are due to Martin Drewe, no longer at Pearson Education but who dispensed valuable advice and encouragement to this first-time author, and to Penelope Allport for tolerating late amendments to the text.

To Ian Johnson I will always be grateful for fixing my troublesome computer gadgetry for no more than the price of a coffee or beer. Finally I thank my wife Eva and daughters Frances and Fiona for their forbearance as I moped around the house on the days when words wouldn't flow.

David Stamp
London, 2002

1

The harsh light
of hindsight

"Those who argue that we are already in a recession, I think, are reasonably certain to be wrong ..."

– Alan Greenspan, Chairman of the Federal Reserve Board, speaking on August 21, 1990 when the US economy was already in a recession[1]

It's easy to sneer at people who make predictions that turn out to be wrong, better still hopelessly wrong. We indulge in a smugness warmed by hindsight, especially when the unfortunate forecaster happens to be an expert. Of course there can be no greater expert on the American economy than Alan Greenspan, Chairman of the mighty Federal Reserve Board. Yet Greenspan, regarded by many as one of the shrewdest figures in global economics, didn't spot a recession even when it was going on around him. Why? And if Greenspan can blunder, what hope is there that lesser mortals might predict a recession a year, or even a month ahead? Research by the International Monetary Fund is not encouraging: it has found that out of 72 recessions worldwide in the 1990s economists foresaw just eight in the year before they happened. Economists, at least the more honest among them, are well aware of the shortcoming of their predictions. "If they are reasonably well done the chances are they will add something to our knowledge but I will not defend them. I know very well that we simply don't forecast too well," says Victor Zarnowitz, one of six "wise men," all senior economists, who declare the start and end of American recessions.[2]

Is this funny or alarming? Shrinking economies are, of course, no laughing matter. When recessions strike wealthy nations hundreds of thousands of people, even millions, lose their jobs, and electorates can vent their anger by voting their political leaders out of power. George Bush Senior led America through the recession that Greenspan failed to spot and a period of high unemployment that followed. For that he paid a high price, losing the 1992 presidential

Is this funny or alarming? Shrinking economies are, of course, no laughing matter.

election to a candidate who campaigned on the simple slogan "It's the economy, stupid." That, of course, was Bill Clinton who subsequently presided over the longest boom in American history.

In poorer nations, where life is precarious at the best of times, recessions are yet worse; they condemn legions of already poor people to a depth of poverty unknown in the wealthy world. In the recession year of 1991 the US economy shrank half a percent, and that followed eight years of uninterrupted growth which had averaged 4 percent annually. Americans emerged from 1991 still immensely wealthier than they had been a decade earlier. In the Third World recessions are often in a different league. For instance the Indonesian economy contracted 13 percent in just one year, 1998, provoking something that the United States hasn't experienced for a long time: food riots. However these events have one depressing thing in common: few people saw them coming until it was too late. Just as the Fed tripped up in 1990, so did another august institution of the global economy, the International Monetary Fund (IMF) a few years later. Well into the preceding year the IMF, along with other forecasters, thought 1998 would be another year of strong growth for Indonesia. Yet only a few months later it had to lead a $47 billion rescue for the country. It's unlikely that anyone in the shantytowns of Jakarta sniggered at this twist of fate.

Forewarned is forearmed

Getting the forecast right matters. If Greenspan had spotted the recession creeping up perhaps the Fed wouldn't have sat on its hands between July and late October 1990, when it finally knuckled down to stimulating the economy with some serious interest rate cuts. It took no less than two years and 17 cuts, which drove its fed funds target from 8 percent down to 3 percent, before Greenspan had revived the economy. As Americans voted in 1992 unemployment was still well over 7 percent, a far cry from the sub-4 percent rate eight years later. Whether Indonesia could have avoided its calamity is debatable but surely a more timely forecast would have better prepared the government, the IMF and everyone else who had to sort out the mess for rapid action. Forewarned is forearmed, after all.

Similarly the stock market has its own tradition of lousy forecasts. Some of the most memorable mis-predictions date from the Wall Street Crash of 1929 when a speculative bubble burst, with hideous consequences for ordinary Americans. Over time a cottage industry has developed in poking fun at the poor souls who were brave, or stupid enough to venture predictions at that time. Again people from respected institutions who we feel ought to have known better make popular targets – with the benefit of hindsight, naturally. Principal among these is one Irving Fisher, a professor of economics at Yale University. This is how he made himself a laughing stock. "Stocks have reached what looks like a permanently high plateau," he said, less than a fortnight before the bottom fell out of Wall Street on October 29, 1929.[3] Undaunted, Fisher predicted in mid-November, 1929 that: "The end of the decline of the stock market will … probably not be long, only a few more days at most." The wait was somewhat longer and the plunge greater. By the time the Dow Jones Industrial Average hit the bottom three years later it had lost 90 percent of its value. Again it's doubtful that many people made light of Fisher's misfortune during the Great Depression which followed the crash.

Only in a prosperous age, decades after the event, can we see the funny side of such predictions. Yet every era produces its own false prophets, not least our own when another stock market bubble burst and helped to pitch the US economy into its first recession in more than a decade. In 1982 the US stock market began its longest bull run in history. After more than a decade when inflation had ravaged stagnant stock prices, the Dow burst through 1000 points and didn't stop – notwithstanding a couple of spectacular but brief "corrections" – until it peaked at above 11,700 points 18 years later. During this time many forecasters who happened to be bullish by temperament made a name for themselves, because the market usually obliged by rising whenever they encouraged investors to buy more stocks. To their devoted followers, many of whom grew rich for a while by following their advice, they seemed to have a magic touch. One such pundit was Mary Meeker, a share analyst at the Wall Street house Morgan Stanley who specialized in high technology companies. The final frantic stages of the bull run were marked by what Greenspan called "irrational exuberance" as investors scrambled for stocks of companies in the high technology business, especially the internet. A number of Wall Street analysts helped to feed this frenzy with stock tips but it was Meeker who became nicknamed "The Queen of the Internet." Many Americans bet their life savings on her recommendations and it was great while it lasted. A bubble inflated and everyone got rich for a while, not least Meeker herself. At the height of high technology mania she is reputed to have made $15 million a year. But bubbles always burst and this one did in March 2000. Fear replaced greed and in the public imagination analysts rapidly turned from heroes into villains as stock prices tumbled. Meeker ended up getting sued, albeit unsuccessfully, for recommending technology stocks even as the market for them collapsed. As with Greenspan's recession a decade earlier, neither Meeker nor her peers realized the world had changed until well after the event.

> **Fear replaced greed and in the public imagination analysts rapidly turned from heroes into villains as stock prices tumbled.**

Flawed forecasters

Sadly the harsh light of hindsight can expose even the most respected or popular figures in economics and finance as flawed forecasters. But do these anecdotes illustrate isolated episodes of bad luck, or a systematic failure of the prediction business? How many economists or market analysts predict the great turning points, when boom turns to bust or vice versa, when citizens prosper or suffer and when investors make a killing or lose their shirts? Whether we live in Manhattan or Jakarta should we trust the Market Prophets; should we believe a word they say?

But first a definition. As the scope of this book is broad that definition is necessarily loose: Market Prophets are people who predict the ups and downs of an economy, a financial market or anything that trades on financial markets – such as stocks, currencies or crude oil – and publish the results. Publication is important. Alan Greenspan is not, strictly speaking, a Market Prophet. Few of his forecasts ever see the light of day and his great mis-prediction of August 1990 came to light only five years later. Luckily for his reputation Greenspan made the comment at a meeting of the Federal Open Market Committee, the Fed body that sets official US interest rates, behind closed doors. Transcripts of the meetings are published so long after the event as to be usually of only historic or academic interest. However, the likes of Fisher and Meeker do qualify as Market Prophets because they stick their necks out by making predictions in public.

Some Market Prophets look at the big picture, tracking entire economies by forecasting the figures which signal their fortunes. Gross domestic product (GDP), which measures a nation's output of goods and services, is a broad indicator of whether an economy is growing or contracting, and at what rate. But economists also predict other indicators which affect the lives of governments, businesses and individuals, such as inflation and unemployment. Other experts forecast market prices, be they for stocks, bonds, currencies, oil, gold or grains. A forecaster can predict averages and indices, such as the Dow or the FTSE 100, which track the overall performance of top companies traded on the New York and London stock markets respectively. As stocks are an entitlement to a share in the future earnings of a company, so an army of analysts predicts those earnings. Analysts also predict prices of the stocks themselves – or at least try to pin down their "fair value" – and controversially recommend whether to buy, hold or sell them.

Straddling the gap between economies and markets are interest rates, which are set by an amalgam of market forces and state diktat. Central banks such as the US Federal Reserve, the European Central Bank (ECB) and the Bank of Japan control short-term interest rates. The Federal Open Market Committee can, without consulting anybody, raise or lower its target for the fed funds rate, which is what commercial banks charge each other for loans overnight. The ECB's benchmark is likewise short term, in this case the minimum rate at which it makes two-week loans to commercial banks in the euro zone. Financial markets can react sharply to changes in official rates so investors and traders await few events with greater anticipation than the regular meetings of central bank policymakers, especially when there's the whiff of a change in the air. But central bankers control only short-term interest rates. Medium and long-term rates, as reflected in the price of bonds issued by governments and corporations for up to 30 years, fluctuate on the markets. Whether the rates are set by the state or the market, there is a Market Prophet out there trying to forecast them.

Market Prophets' predictions also range from the ultra short term to the long term. An economist will forecast a monthly inflation figure to be released the next day as much as what the inflation rate will be in a couple of years' time.

The feel good factor

So the prediction business falls into these rough categories of economies and markets, with interest rates in both. Each influences the others and therefore many of the forecasts feed into each other. National, regional and global economies affect – and are affected by – markets. If investors believe the US economy will grow strongly, and consequently companies' profits are likely to rise, they will buy up stocks and the market will rise. The influence can flow in the opposite direction: major shifts on the markets can stimulate or subdue the wider economy. For instance the stock boom of the 1990s created a "feel good factor" among Americans. As the value of their stock investments soared they went on a spending spree, even if they hadn't sold the shares to turn a paper profit into hard cash. Feeling rich was good enough. As consumer spending accounts for almost two-thirds of US GDP the effect was electrifying: in the second half of the 1990s the economy grew on average more than 4 percent a year. At the same time Europe struggled to achieve half that rate and Japan dipped in and out of recession. Naturally it ended in tears: many US corporations also got carried away, frittering away huge sums on high technology investments which produced few profits and a lot of losses. Everyone woke up to reality when the stock bubble burst. Ordinary Americans moderated their shopping habits and corporations slashed their investment spending. As a result America went into recession in March 2001.

So sometimes the dog wags its tail, sometimes the tail wags the dog. Anyone forecasting the economy should build in predictions of market prices, and anyone predicting market prices or company earnings should build in forecasts of the economy. This is, at least, the view of the fundamentalists, the school of forecasters which believes that real events and value ultimately determine market prices, even if they do overshoot or undershoot at times. Fundamentalists accept that psychology plays a role: investors can get irrationally exuberant and there is no better example than the technology mania. Conversely they sometimes become excessively gloomy. Perhaps history will prove that the stock market dive after September 11, 2001 was an example of overselling. Fundamentalists will note how prices bounced back within a few weeks of the suicide hijackings, showing how logic and the underlying value of shares reassert themselves. But another school of forecasters, the technical analysts, believes that psychology is

Greed drives investors to buy during booms even when logic suggests that it's too good to be true, and fear drives them to dump stocks during slumps, even when logic suggests things can't be that bad.

a major motivator of markets. Greed drives investors to buy during booms even when logic suggests that it's too good to be true, and fear drives them to dump stocks during slumps, even when logic suggests things can't be that bad. The relatively small but pugnacious band of technical analysts asserts that the best way to predict is not to study the economy or profitability of a company, but to analyze graphs of past stock price trends, find patterns and apply them to the future. The schism between these two denominations is covered in Chapter 9.

Job opportunities

Job opportunities for Market Prophets are good, at least in prosperous times. They work in the government and private sectors, at international organizations and at universities. In government every finance ministry or treasury department has its team of economists; so do central banks, most of which enjoy independence in setting interest rates. Forecasts are key to good monetary policy decisions: while changes in rates can affect markets instantly, they take months or years to influence the wider economy so central bankers look well into the future. Teams are large. For instance, the Bank of England's Chief Economist, Charlie Bean, heads a division of 120, although not all of them forecast. The Federal Reserve system employs a couple of hundred economists, split roughly equally between its Washington headquarters and regional Federal Reserve banks based in a dozen cities around the United States.

How much of forecasters' work that sees the light of day varies. The Bank of England reveals its view of the future in a quarterly report which includes detailed forecasts of inflation and GDP up to two years ahead. The Bank has a target of keeping inflation to 2.5 percent, so economists in the markets scrutinize these projections for clues on how its Monetary Policy Committee may change interest rates to hit the target. Other central banks have been less enthusiastic about revealing their predictions but the Bank of Japan now publishes them regularly. The European Central Bank, which controls interest rates for the 12 nations that use the euro, has yielded to pressure to release economic projections but they appear only twice a year. Likewise the Federal Reserve is reluctant to reveal its forecasts too often. In-house economists prepare them six times a year but they are sent to Congress only once every six months.

International organizations such as the International Monetary Fund in Washington and the Paris-based Organization for Economic Cooperation and Development (OECD) are major forecasters. The IMF produces a global report twice a year, a mammoth exercise including predictions of economies great and small from America to Armenia. Academics also predict economies and markets, and much of the research into improving the accuracy of forecasting goes on in universities. Research institutes, private and state-funded, play a leading role in the economic life of many nations. Germany has a number, the best known of which is the Munich-based Ifo institute. Ifo also conducts a survey which is a key indicator of German economic trends.

Among the biggest prediction factories are the commercial banks and brokerages – usually under the same roof these days – which produce reams of research on everything from the economy to company earnings. Players in this game include the Wall Street giants such as JP Morgan Chase, Merrill Lynch, Goldman Sachs and Morgan Stanley, the big European names such as Swiss-owned UBS Warburg, Deutsche Bank of Germany and HSBC of Britain, plus Tokyo houses like Nomura and Daiwa, although the Japanese presence is much reduced internationally from its heyday in the 1980s due to a banking crisis at home. Big banks don't only sell services to clients. They are major traders on their own account of stocks, bonds, currencies and the derivatives that spring from them, such as futures and options. Often analysts and economists feed forecasts to traders at their own bank but their main work lies outside. Their research is dished out to clients usually at no extra charge beyond the fat fees for banking and brokerage services. In format it ranges from glossy brochures and smart password-protected websites to brief e-mails giving rapid analysis of economic statistics just released, interest rate decisions just made and company earnings just announced.

Conflicts of interest

Banking and brokerage houses are known as "the sell side" because selling shares is their chief business. The biggest clients for brokerage services are fund management companies and insurers on "the buy side." Fund managers have two major lines of business: mutual funds (known in Britain as unit trusts) and pension funds.

Banking and brokerage houses are known as "the sell side" because selling shares is their chief business.

With mutual funds private savers entrust their money to professionals who invest it on their behalf, the idea being that their superior experience and knowledge of the markets will produce superior returns. The other half of the business involves investing the savings of employees pooled in their company pension fund to produce reliable income for their retirement. The sums involved are staggering. For instance at the end of September 2001 Boston-based Fidelity Investments managed more than $800 billion in assets, even though share markets had just tumbled due to the attacks on America. Insurers are likewise major players on the stock and bonds markets, investing their premium income to fund the claims they have to pay out.

Fund managers have traditionally relied on their brokers for research and forecasts, although they don't pay for it. The cost is bundled in with brokerage fees but the fund managers pass them on to their clients. So it's private savers and the occupational pension funds that end up paying many of the Market Prophets' salaries. Whoever pays the bills, fund managers have become increasingly unhappy with the quality of research offered by brokers in recent years. It has to do with the fact that brokerage houses have a separate line of business: investment banking. Organizing company takeovers, mega mergers, privatizations and stock market flotations is lucrative work. But the boom years of the 1990s raised conflicts of interest between investment banking and research departments on Wall Street and elsewhere. Could an analyst publicly slam a dot.com company while colleagues down the corridor were organizing its stock market launch? Would an analyst make a gloomy forecast for a blue chip corporation while investment bankers at the same firm were vying to handle its next takeover bid? At times analysts seemed just another member of the sales team, an allegation levelled against Meeker (and denied). Whatever the truth many fund managers have built their own research teams in a quest for analysis and forecasts untainted by conflicts of interest.

Forecasters

Another arm of the prediction business is companies which specialize in selling economic and financial forecasts plus analysis without any of the baggage of broking or banking. One of the best known is Wharton Econometric Forecasting Associates (WEFA), which was founded in 1963 by Lawrence Klein, a professor at the University of Pennsylvania. Links exist not only between specialist forecasting groups and academia. For instance the Fed Chairman was once a principal of an economic forecasting firm, Townsend-Greenspan & Co. Finally there are newsletters which economists and market watchers fax, mail and e-mail to subscribers. These cover a wide variety of topics from hard forecasts and stock tips to more general thought-provoking articles and research. Subscribing to them isn't like getting *Time* magazine or *The Economist*. Typically a subscription costs the better part of $2000 a year.

It's hard to say how large the forecasting industry is. But *Nelson's Directory of Investment Research*, a US trade publication, lists 17,000 stock analysts alone worldwide, not to mention the armies of economists – although by no means all are forecasters. Many big corporations have their own in-house forecasters but often we don't hear much from them. Their work largely confined to the company memo and report, advising managers on the state

> **To qualify as a Market Prophet, you must be visible.**

of the economies and markets where they must make business decisions. Therefore they fall outside the scope of this book because to qualify as a Market Prophet, you must be visible.

The age of the pundit

Market Prophets are, willingly or unwillingly, more visible than ever. State institutions such as central banks may not always be keen to reveal their forecasts but the pressure for greater accountability and transparency is forcing them to emerge from the shadows. In the private sector the attitude is often the opposite: publicity is a virtue. The forecaster is the public face of many organizations. Ask average Americans to name the boss of Morgan Stanley and they may well be stumped for an answer. Ask them who Morgan Stanley's internet analyst is, and they may well name her. For banks, great and small, a two-minute television appearance by their chief economist or technology analyst equates to hundreds of thousands, possibly millions of dollars in free advertising. Why? Because we all love a good forecast – at least we hope it'll turn out to be good – and the media know it.

We live in the age of the pundit; explosive growth of the media in the past decade has created an enormous demand for expert opinion and prediction. Few of us can resist a tempting forecast, especially if it touches our career, happiness or our wealth. Who can show the patience of Albert Einstein, who said: "I never think of the future, it comes soon enough."?[4] So great is this fascination with the future that sometimes the forecast can eclipse the event itself. Kenneth Clarke discovered this, to his irritation, while running the British economy as Chancellor of the Exchequer from 1993–1997. "Some of the forecasts would make big news. It used to really annoy me that occasionally forecasts would make number one or two item in the national news when what was actually happening in the economy was making no news at all," he says.[5]

Whether we are savers or borrowers, large or small, it would be nice to know what's going to happen before taking the plunge.

In few areas of life are we bombarded more by predictions, solicited and otherwise, than in finance and the economy. Whether we are savers or borrowers, large or small, it would be nice to know what's going to happen before taking the plunge. Every decision raises questions about the future, regardless of whether it's taken personally, by a business or by a state. In our personal lives we may ask what's the stock market going to do. Should we put our savings into shares or leave them in a relatively safe but unrewarding bank account? Will interest rates rise or fall? Should we take out a fixed rate or a floating rate mortgage to buy a new home? Should we buy a new home at all, or will there be a recession in which I lose my job? On the wholesale financial markets the sums of money are greater but the decisions are often similar. At times of uncertainty even fund managers have to balance the risks of the stock market against the low returns of the deposit account. In business no corporation will build a factory or launch a new service without weighing the risks in the years ahead; the ebb and flow of the economy can make the difference between a profitable venture and a commercial disaster. Finally there are governments and central banks which simultaneously guide the economy and are hostages to it. They set policies to stimulate or slow the economy, but the economy can bite back. A recession can turn a healthy budget surplus into a yawning deficit, or a likely election victory into an ignominious defeat. An unforeseen boom can wreck a carefully laid interest rate policy by igniting inflation. All these questions, decisions and dilemmas demand one thing: a forecast.

Events, dear boy, events

In 1789 Benjamin Franklin wrote to a friend: "In this world nothing can be said to be certain, except death and taxes." Forecasters can add a third certainty in their lives: the Unexpected Event. Sooner or later a bolt will descend from the blue which is guaranteed to upset the best predictions. Of course surprises are not unique to the economy or financial markets. "Events, dear boy, events," is how Harold Macmillan, a patrician British Prime Minister of the 1950s and 1960s, responded when asked to name the biggest problem in political life. Who foresaw the collapse of communism? Certainly not Erich Honecker, the East German leader who predicted in spring 1989 that the Berlin Wall would stand 100 years. Within a few months the Wall had fallen and a year later the entire East German state had followed suit. Who predicted that suicide hijackers would snuff out thousands of lives on September 11, 2001?

Such events, while thankfully rarely as horrifying as the felling of the World Trade Center, make the job of economic and financial forecasters particularly difficult. In the prediction business they're known as Exogenous Shocks. It may be possible, if not now then sometime in the future as the science improves, to predict reasonably accurately the internal forces of an economy or a market. But can any forecaster, however gifted, foresee a shock from the outside?

Can any forecaster, however gifted, foresee a shock from the outside?

Peter Bernstein, a veteran economist and Wall Street historian, believes that exogenous shocks push forecasting beyond the line that divides difficulty from impossibility. A few years ago he reviewed past economic and market forecasts he had made according to various scenarios of high inflation, low inflation and so on. The range of forecasts was wide and the chances of being right consequently greater. "Although I thought I had done them very carefully and the range of scenarios I had described was wide, too many observations came outside the range. I just decided I can't forecast. Period. I just don't believe that we understand the range of what can happen," he says. "The world is too complex, and there are so many shocks. We don't know the future and we should manage our affairs accordingly."[6]

Undoubtedly September 11 delivered the most stunning shock to the United States since World War Two. The US stock market remained closed for almost a week but when it reopened the Dow dived nearly 15 percent in a matter of days before, almost as surprisingly, it recovered all those losses by early November. Naturally no one saw this coming. How could you expect any Market Prophet to do so when the mighty intelligence apparatus of the United States failed to predict such a shocking attack? How can forecasters predict economies and markets which may merely be passively responding to events determined by soldiers, politicians and suicide hijackers?

Shocks don't necessarily come from outside the economy or markets. Americans may regard the late 1990s as years of prosperity but few people in East Asia, Latin America or Eastern Europe look back on them as a golden age, again thanks to an unexpected event, or phenomenon. This time it was contagion. When countries in the Far East ran into trouble, investors took fright and pulled their money out of markets across the developing world. One by one nations from Thailand to Indonesia and from Russia to Brazil, which had little in common beyond the fact they were developing economies, hit deep trouble. Again, few people foresaw this economic domino effect.

A healthy and intelligent skepticism

Yet the Market Prophets keep forecasting and we keep listening to them, or even act on their predictions. Some have built their careers on a few correct calls which elevated them to the status of guru, bringing them fame and wealth. But is this due to skill or luck? Is making a good prediction yesterday any guarantee that a

forecaster won't blunder tomorrow? If I made a small fortune following a forecaster's advice last year, what's to say I won't lose a bigger
fortune this year? Can anyone know in advance who'll make the
best predictions, rather than after
the event when it's too late to act on
them? Do the best-known forecasters, whether it be the IMF or Mary
Meeker, necessarily make the best
forecasters? Any review of forecasting accuracy will show up individuals
who outperform the pack, the major-
ity of Market Prophets who huddle around what is misleadingly
known as the "consensus" forecast. But if you compile a list of the
outperformers do the same names keep cropping up over time?
Ken Clarke thinks not. As Chancellor he was so dissatisfied with
Treasury forecasts that he studied figures produced by outside economists in the City of London. "It was the outliers again and again
who turned out to be right," he says. "Sadly it was never the same
people who were right every time – which is why you should treat all
forecasts with a healthy and intelligent skepticism."

Some have built their careers on a few correct calls which elevated them to the status of guru, bringing them fame and wealth.

This book will explore how the Market Prophets go about their
work, and whether Clarke is right to regard it with a healthy and
intelligent skepticism.

Notes

1 Greenspan was addressing the Federal Open Market Committee,
   which sets official US interest rates. Transcripts of the meetings are
   released after five years, hence this was published in 1995. It is
   available on www.federalreserve.gov

2 Interview with author.

3 Quoted in *The Experts Speak*, by Christopher Cerf and Victor Navasky. This "Definitive Compendium of Authoritative Misinformation," which has an entire section on the Wall Street Crash, pops up in the bibliography of some serious academic studies of the accuracy of economic and market forecasts.

4 Interview, 1930.

5 Interview with author.

6 Interview with author.

2

Dismal science, dismal record?

"If economists could manage to get themselves thought of as humble, competent people on a level with dentists, that would be splendid."

– John Maynard Keynes, *Essays in Persuasion*, 1931

One hundred and fifty years ago the Scottish essayist Thomas Carlyle called economists "Respectable Professors of the Dismal Science" and this epithet, at least the latter part of it, has stuck. But why should economists struggle even to achieve a reputation for

"Respectable Professors of the Dismal Science"

humble competence? Why do they rank below dentists in public esteem, as suggested by John Maynard Keynes, the father of modern economic thought? Victor Zarnowitz, who has studied the record of economists since the 1960s, believes it's all about forecasting. "The ability to produce accurate predictions of the course of the economy in the near term future is probably the main criterion by which the public judges the usefulness of our entire profession," he wrote.[1]

In fact forecasting is only part of the economist's job and macro economists, who study entire economies, are only part of the profession. Micro economists, who sift the nitty-gritty of supply and demand, can make you rich without offering a single prediction. A few years ago the British government discovered this when it hired two micro economists, Professors Ken Binmore of University College London and Paul Klemperer of Nuffield College Oxford, to design an auction of licenses for the next generation of mobile phone services. It was a stunning success. An exercise that had been expected to raise a few billion pounds at most turned into a bonanza for the government and taxpayer. After almost eight weeks and 150 rounds of bidding in the spring of 2000 telecoms companies paid a staggering £22.5 billion for the five licences – almost £400 for every man, woman and child in Britain.

But it isn't experts in games theory, such as Binmore and Klemperer, who shape public views on the economics profession. It is those who predict. Forecasters stir emotions in a way that the rest of the profession rarely does. Everyone loves the forecaster who gets it right and loathes the one who gets it wrong, especially when a lot of money is involved. That goes not only for economists but also the armies of analysts tackling financial markets, particularly the stock market where most private investors bet their savings. In the boom years of the late 1990s the top stock analysts, such as Mary Meeker, became American folk heroes because they made investors rich for a while by telling them to buy. When the bubble burst the lawsuits began to fly and adoration turned to anger.

> **It isn't experts in games theory who shape public views on the economics profession. It is those who predict.**

"The 1990s are going to be very difficult"

It's not hard to find examples of remarkable success and failure simply by looking into the archives. On December 22, 1989 Cal Mankowski, a Wall Street reporter at Reuters, reported on what economists and stock market gurus expected to happen in the coming decade. While some forecasts proved spot on, others were a little wide of the mark. In the article, Hugh Johnson of First Albany Corporation said: "We're very close to recession and it could start in the third quarter of 1990." Full marks to Johnson, who is chairman of First Albany's fund management arm, for predicting what Alan Greenspan did not: the recession that began in August 1990. The report also quoted Byron Wien, a Wall Street veteran at Morgan Stanley. Back at the end of 1989 he was similarly down-beat. "The 1980s was the best decade in the history of the world for stocks and bonds together," he said. "The 1990s are going to be very difficult." By looking further ahead Wien, a Chicago orphan who worked his way up from an office boy at the Pabst brewing company, proved to be as wrong as Johnson was right in making a gloomy forecast. Hindsight shows that he got the opening years of the decade right but couldn't have been more wrong for the rest of the 1990s. Indeed 1990 and 1991 were very difficult but once the economy had got over the recession it embarked on ten years of uninterrupted growth, the longest expansion in American history. The stock market followed a similar pattern. At first Wien was right to be pessimistic as share prices fell sharply in 1990. But most long-term bull markets have at least one temporary downturn and this one was no exception: 1990 turned out to be a short-lived blip in the great bull market which lasted from 1982 to 2000. On the day Mankowski ran his story in 1989 the Dow Jones

BOX 2.1
·············

It's all in the stars

Missed a recession? Predicted a bull run the day before the market crashed? Perhaps it's time to shut down the economic model and look to the heavens. If people can have horoscopes why not stocks? Enter astroeconomics, which uses astrological cycles to predict markets or, more precisely, the behavior of people who buy and sell on the markets. "The moon and the sun have the power to move the oceans across many thousands of miles," said David Simpson, who has analyzed the stock market for forty years. "The average human body is made up at least 87 percent of water and is subject to the same tidal flows. These magnetic attractions cause a chemical and neurological reaction within the body which changes peoples' perception of black and white."[1]

Astroeconomics and its related mystic disciplines are not uncommon in finance. In the late 1980s an elderly restaurateur called Nui Onoue conned Japanese banks out of 269 billion yen (more than $2 billion) to punt on the stock market. Onoue, also known as The Dark Lady of Osaka, held regular Sunday seances for brokers where she would intone "The price will rise ... buy now!" before a Buddhist statue. She became one of the biggest players on the Tokyo market but fell when it crashed in the early 1990s. She wasn't alone. When the scandal broke the chairman of the Industrial Bank of Japan, which suffered most of the losses, resigned in disgrace. Onoue was convicted of fraud in 1998 and got a hefty prison sentence.

Perhaps Onoue should have tried to connect with Henry Weingarten, who runs The Astrologers Fund in New York (motto: "Always a stellar performance!"). "We called the Tokyo market crash two and half years in advance to the day. We have a record like that; we're incredibly specific, accurate and precise," he said.[2] Weingarten takes a catholic approach to prediction. "We're not always right, but we're more right than anything else. We do fundamental analysis, technical analysis and we do financial astrology ... Some of it's astrology, some of it isn't but we put it all together." Weingarten studies the stars from a Manhattan office cluttered with heaps of horoscopes and a couple of fish tanks – there for the good feng shui. His work has attracted a lot of attention, not all of it welcome. In October 2001 the Securities and Exchange Commission filed civil charges against Weingarten alleging he had participated in a stock manipulation scam. A few months later he settled out of court but earned a censure from the SEC. None of this subdued Weingarten's enthusiasm for playing the market. Speaking in an interview at the end of October 2001 he boasted of his latest stock investment, presumably dictated by the stars. "Yesterday (it) was being dumped at $11.10; we bought it. It's $12.70 today ... It's going to close at $13." That stock was Enron. Within a few weeks the energy giant had collapsed and the stock was worth 26 cents. The search for the foolproof forecasting technique continues.

1 Quoted in a Reuters feature by my colleague Hament Bulsara which was published on March 13, 2001. I have drawn on the article for this piece.
2 Interview with author on October 31, 2001.

Industrial Average closed at 2711 points. A decade later he was still at his post to report that the Dow finished 1999 just short of 11,500, having more than quadrupled in the meantime. Some difficult decade.

To be fair Wien's pessimism paid off a decade later. Every New Year he lists 10 surprises which have a better than 50–50 chance of happening in the coming 12 months. For 2000 he predicted the internet would finally meet its Waterloo. "There is a graduated car-nage in technology issues. Some internet content and retailing stocks correct 50 percent and access providers come down by a third," he predicted. "Hardware and personal computer makers with current earnings decline only 25 percent. The internet continues to be viewed as the most powerful business phenomenon in our lifetime, but the stocks were discounting a profitability reality that was unlikely to come true." Spot on this time.

Back in 1989, Tokyo forecasters proved to be well wide of the mark but in a mirror image of their American colleagues: here excessive optimism clouded the crystal ball. "We see good growth in the Japanese economy over the next 10 years with increased corporate profit margins," said analyst Pelham Smithers at the investment bank Shearson Lehman Hutton in Tokyo. Smithers forecast Tokyo's Nikkei stock average could rise 10 to 12 percent a year in the 1990s. Such a prediction would scarcely have raised any eyebrows at the time, given that the Nikkei had gained on average about 15 percent a year for two decades. What neither Smithers nor most other Japan watchers realized at the time was that they were peering into a bubble about to burst: within a few days the Nikkei hit a peak of 38,915 points which, more than a decade later, remains a distant dream. Within little more than two years the Nikkei had crashed 50 percent and that wasn't the end of it: by the end of 2001 it had lost almost three quarters of its value. Far from a decade of good growth and bigger profits Japan spent much of the 1990s slipping in and out of recession, its banking industry mired in crisis.

Nigel Lawson's troublesome forecasts

Bad predictions can lead to disaster. In the late 1980s the British Treasury seriously underestimated the rates of economic growth and inflation. Whether due to bad forecasts or old-fashioned bad judgment, the then Chancellor of the Exchequer Nigel Lawson made a series of blunders which tipped Britain into a recession. Ironically Lawson's mistakes began in 1987 when he feared that a sudden dive on stock markets around the world would do just that – trigger a recession. So he steadily cut interest rates (this was almost ten years before politicians handed control of monetary policy to the Bank of England) to their lowest level in a decade in 1988. Lawson added fuel to the fire in March that year with a radical tax-cutting budget. The economy began to grow strongly, too strongly in fact. In 1988 GDP grew 5.2 percent, well over double its long-term average and far more than the economy could handle without serious overheating. Inflation took off and Lawson was forced into an about-face, jacking interest rates up to a sky-high 15 percent. It was all too much for the economy which suffered a boom and a bust in quick succession that haunts chancellors to this day. By the time Lawson quit in 1989 in a row with Prime Minister Margaret Thatcher the economy was heading for recession.

Just as bad workmen blame their tools, bad chancellors may blame their forecasts. Ken Clarke, Lawson's successor-but-two, is highly critical of projections served up by Treasury economists but believes that they alone cannot explain Lawson's mistakes. "They had completely screwed up both forecasting and policy at the end of the 1980s … The Treasury forecasts were particularly bad in 1987–1988. But in the end what took Nigel over the edge of the cliff was an overreaction in policy terms," says Clarke. "Given that all forecasting is uncertain I'm afraid I did think that the Treasury's record before I arrived had been particularly poor, and it didn't get much better when I was there."[2]

Just as bad workmen blame their tools, bad chancellors may blame their forecasts.

Clarke's term was dominated by two considerations: cutting a budget deficit which demanded government borrowing of £1 billion a week in 1993, and restoring his Conservative Party's reputation for competence in running the economy. Another disaster had struck in 1992 when speculators on the currency market, led by the US financier George Soros, ejected sterling from the exchange rate mechanism, a system designed to keep European Union currencies stable against each other. With the opposition Labour Party gaining popularity under its new leader, Tony Blair, Clarke's only hope was to get the economy growing as fast as possible without overheating and pushing up inflation again. That meant keeping interest rates as low as possible to stimulate growth and, hopefully, a "feel good factor" among British voters.

Clarke, now a backbench parliamentarian after a failed run at the Conservative leadership in 2001, feels that Treasury forecasters got in the way. "They were constantly advocating very hawkish monetary policy because they continually overestimated the risk of inflation," he says. "As far as the public finances were concerned, they carried on with the historic error they've always made of underestimating the growth of revenues when the economy is doing well, just as they overestimate the revenues once the economy starts to turn down. That was the record in the 1980s which got Nigel Lawson into such trouble."

Just as inflation forecasts are vital for setting interest rates, so are economic growth forecasts for estimating government revenue and spending. Tax revenue rises and falls in tandem with the economy; when growth drops or vanishes state income can plummet just as social spending such as on unemployment benefits goes through the roof. But it wasn't just the British Treasury that made this kind of mistake. Underestimating growth and overestimating inflation was a common fault among forecasters in the 1990s in the United States and Britain where reforms seem to have made their economies more efficient and able to grow faster without stoking inflation Lawson-style. This "New Economy" phenomenon was still controversial, and remains so. Clarke recalls much to-ing and fro-ing with his officials over the forecasts. "I used to enjoy these arguments. We used to have long debates and then we would produce a figure which the Treasury and myself could both live with."

Fire the forecasters?

Notwithstanding these compromises Clarke began comparing the track record of Treasury forecasters with that of their peers, and came up with a radical idea that horrified the Mandarins of Whitehall. "You could make comparisons in which the Treasury wasn't the worst but it was certainly a very indifferent performer," he says. "I made arrangements for the forecasting team to be given a fixed-term contract. I wished to put [forecasting] out to competitive tender and decide whether or not we kept it in-house or whether we recruited some economic think-tank to do the forecasting for us," he says. During 18 years in power Conservative governments privatized numerous institutions from British Telecom to the railways, but economic forecasting was not destined to be one of them. "This was regarded with total horror by the department who nevertheless acknowledged it was my policy. We agreed a time when it

Clarke came up with a radical idea that horrified the Mandarins of Whitehall.

would be done which, in the event, turned out to be after the election." Blair won the general election of May 1, 1997 by a landslide and Ken Clarke's plan to put economic forecasting out to tender died with the Conservative government.

The future as we don't know it

Is the forecasting record of private sector economists any better? Peter Bernstein, who has 50 years' experience of the business, has examined not only his own predictions for the US economy but those of his fellow forecasters. Sadly he has found them often to be a more reliable indicator of the past than the future.

For many years Bernstein contributed to the Blue Chip forecast, a regular survey of 50 or so experts in the prediction business. He recalls, with less than unalloyed pride, his forecasts for 1982 which he made in the autumn of the previous year. For three years running US inflation had been in double digits and contributors to the Blue Chip survey thought it would stay that way in 1982 – except Bernstein, who stuck his neck out by predicting a drop to 8 percent. In fact inflation fell like a stone to 6.2 percent in 1982, thanks to a nasty recession. Bernstein's prediction was wrong, but because the others were even more wrong he took the prize for best forecast of the year. "I won $5000 for this in non-taxable 1982 dollars, which was very nice," he says.[3] Less nice is the conclusion to be drawn from this story. "When change set in, which is when it really mattered, none of us could conceive of how big the change was going to be, from double digit inflation to a very acceptable rate in 12 months. It took a hell of a big recession to pull it down there – but everybody underestimated the decline in

GDP too," he says. "We know very little about the future. If the future is going to look like the present we look smart and if it isn't we look stupid. What we really get paid for is to call the turning points, and the best of us can't do it."

Economic and political anecdote is all very well but passing judgment on the Market Prophets demands objective analysis of the numbers. So Bernstein set out to determine how well economists foresaw the abrupt end of the US economic boom in 2000–2001. As the title of his report suggests – "The Future as We Don't Know It"[4] – the analysis seems to corroborate the anecdote. Bernstein plotted a graph of the average predictions for US industrial production in 2001 that the Blue Chip forecasters had made from January 2000 to April 2001. Then he superimposed the actual rate of industrial production in the same period (Figure 2.1). In their defense it must be said that the forecasters did predict that the frantic growth rates of over 6 percent during much of 2000 would slow the following year and Bernstein tosses them a small bouquet for that. But they still forecast growth of well over 3 percent even though the storm clouds were gathering: the Nasdaq share market, home of the hottest high technology stocks, had begun a meltdown in March 2000 that helped to pitch America into recession a year later. Only after the growth rate of industrial production began tumbling in the autumn of 2000 did the experts start to cut their forecasts. Figure 2.1 clearly shows how the line representing the forecasts follows, rather than leads, the actual rate down. In other words the "predictions" lagged

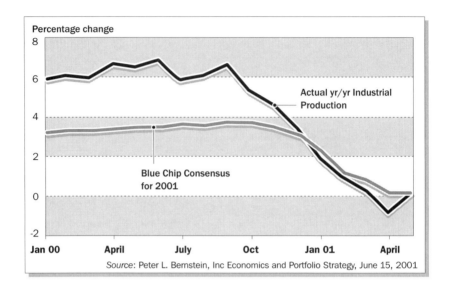

Figure 2.1 *Blue Chip consensus forecast of US industrial production for 2001 versus actual year-on-year percentage change*

events in the real world. "Is this forecasting – or reporting?" asked Bernstein. This failure is best summed up by a quotation from Eugene Ionescu's 1959 play *Le Rhinoceros*: "Tu ne prevois les événements que lorsqu'ils sont déjà arrivés." "You predict events only when they've already happened."

A dose of alchemy

Are market forecasters any better? Not, it seems, on the foreign exchange market, the world's biggest, where on an average day $1.2 trillion in the world's currencies is bought and sold. Some of the transactions are linked to world trade. If an airline in continental Europe, for instance, buys a jet from Boeing of the United States it must sell euros for dollars to make the purchase. But most currency trade is speculative which makes the market volatile and, dare we say it, unpredictable. "Forecasting foreign exchange takes skill, patience and a dose of alchemy," said Rudiger Dornbusch, a professor at the Massachusetts Institute of Technology. A relatively small number of big banks dominate the market but events are felt far more widely. Foreseeing turning points in the value of currencies is critical for everyone from company managers and investors to governments and central banks setting economic and interest rate policies. Or it would be if anybody could manage it.

In June 2001 the US investment bank Lehman Brothers published an assessment of currency forecasting, the title of which is self-explanatory. Its snappy headline, borrowed for this chapter, was "Dismal Science – Dismal Record" (without a question mark).[5] Rather than looking at predictions of an economy, the Lehman Brothers study analyzes forecasts of a market and yet the conclusions are depressingly similar to Bernstein's. "The forecasts are clearly a lagging indicator of the spot rate and they miss all the most important turning points," said Giovanni Pillitteri, co-author of the report.

Lehman Brothers, which excluded its own forecasts from the sample, based the study on a monthly poll conducted by Reuters in which around 50 banks forecast where the euro, yen and pound will stand against the dollar in one, three, six and twelve months' time. The raw materials were median forecasts – the middle number when all the predictions are laid out in order of magnitude – from the polls taken from 1997 to mid-2001. The results were not encouraging. Participants in the poll struggled even to predict correctly whether the currencies would rise or fall, let alone by how much. If you flip a coin to forecast direction, for instance with heads predicting a rise and tails a fall, over time you will be right 50 percent of the time purely by chance. Unfortunately the research showed that the forecasters rarely achieved this modicum of success (Table 2.1).

Currency	1 month ahead	3 months ahead	6 months ahead
euro/dollar	40.48	35.71	38.10
dollar/yen	52.38	45.24	40.48
euro/yen	45.24	38.46	35.71
euro/sterling	42.86	38.10	35.71
sterling/dollar	61.90	52.38	50.00

Source: Lehman Brothers

Table 2.1 *Percentage of median forecasts from Reuters foreign exchange polls 1997–2001 which correctly predicted the direction of currency moves*

Most of the time forecasters would have been better off flipping the coin to decide their prediction, shutting down the computer and heading early for home. One consistent exception was sterling's exchange rate against the dollar, but only because it was unusually stable for most of the study period. On one rate, the euro against the dollar, the forecasters consistently forecast a recovery and consistently got it wrong. By the time the study had been published the euro had lost 28 percent against the dollar since its launch at the start of 1999.[6]

Analysis by Hament Bulsara at Reuters confirms that currency forecasts, like Blue Chip forecasts of US industrial production, shed more light on the past than the future. Figure 2.2 is a graph of the average forecast of the euro against the dollar one month ahead,

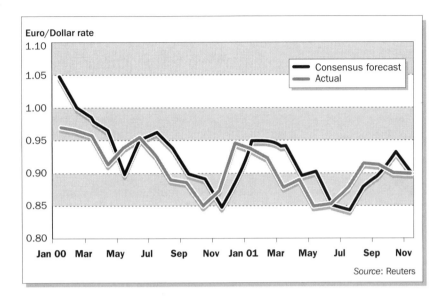

Figure 2.2 *Average economists' forecasts of euro exchange rate against dollar in 2000–2001 compared with actual rate*

taken from Reuters polls in 2000 and 2001, set against the actual rates. Again the "predictions" clearly lag rather than lead the ups and downs of the exchange rate.

Stick to your guns!

As always some individual forecasters did better than the pack as represented by the average but, as with economic predictions, it's rarely the same names that head the league tables from month to month. Sometimes currency forecasters would be better off sticking to their guns, even when the market seems to be turning against them. In January 2000 the beleaguered euro was enjoying a rally above the psychological "parity" level of $1.0 and many forecasters thought that it had finally turned the corner after a long slide the previous year. In the Reuters poll that month the median forecast was for the euro to end the year 2000 at $1.13. However Tony Norfield, head of global treasury research at the Dutch-owned bank ABN Amro, didn't share the pack's optimism. He predicted that far from recovering, it would close 2000 at 95 US cents and he was right. The euro's rally petered out in mid-January and it duly ended the year at 94.22 cents. So the pack's prediction was wrong by 20 percent and Norfield was as near to spot on as you will ever get. But the story doesn't end there. The euro dived faster in 2000 than anyone had expected and fell below Norfield's 95 cents already in April. For a while he stuck to his guns but as the euro sank deeper into the morass he cut his year-end forecast to 83 cents. Again the rate proved right but the timing wrong. In October the euro indeed slumped to 83 cents but the year still had a couple of months to run – and an unexpected event was in store. The market was about to turn in favor of the euro and against Norfield.

> **Sometimes currency forecasters would be better off sticking to their guns, even when the market seems to be turning against them.**

The leading industrial nations, alarmed by the slide, came to the euro's rescue with a lightning raid on the currency market. Out of the blue central banks of the Group of Seven countries[7] scooped up $6 billion worth of euros in a raid that caught currency dealers on the hop. The euro executed a volte face and by the end of the year it had bounced back almost to 95 cents – Norfield's original forecast but one that he had subsequently ditched. Perhaps it's unfair to single him out because few other forecasters could say they did any better and most did a lot worse. At the very least ABN Amro warned its clients at the start of the year that the euro had much further to fall, something that few of its competitors can have done. Nevertheless the moral of the story is that if Norfield had stuck by his original forecasts and ignored the rates flashing up on his trading screen he would have scored a bull's eye. As it was he missed the target by more than 12 percent.

Like comedy, it's all about timing

Norfield was right on the euro's level – not once but twice – but wrong on the timing. The trouble is that in forecasting both elements count. "Like comedy, it's all about timing," says Peter Osler, an economist at GNI, a London futures trader and broker. But perhaps the biggest problem for currency forecasters is that the goalposts keep moving: perceptions of the true value of a currency, and how to calculate it, change frequently. Traditional economics suggest that a major factor influencing the exchange rate of two currencies is the difference in their respective interest rates. If, for instance, the European Central Bank (ECB) cuts interest rates by half a percent-age point, and the US Federal Reserve leaves its unchanged, investments in euros become less attractive relative to those in dol-lars. Therefore the euro's value against the dollar should fall. Sometimes this is indeed the case but the collective thinking of the markets can execute a flip-flop. In the late 1990s the currency market decided to focus on economic growth and "capital flows." From 1996 to 2000 the US economy grew on average more than

4 percent a year while Germany, France and Italy, which collectively account for 70 percent of the euro zone economy, managed only half that. Stock markets either side of the Atlantic reflected this economic disparity. For most of the time continental European markets failed to keep pace with a Wall Street gripped by technology mania. Naturally many European investors sold euros to buy dollars so they could participate in the American great boom, either through the stock market or by buying up US companies directly. This turned traditional economic thinking on its head: if an ECB rate cut could stimulate the European economy, it should slow the flood of capital across the Atlantic and boost, not weaken, the euro's exchange rate. Economists blamed the euro's long decline on Europe's failure to match the American success story, yet when the US economy screeched to a halt in 2001 the euro's "recovery" was disappointing. From a low point of around 84 US cents in July 2001 it staggered back to 92 cents in the following couple of months – a far cry from its launch at $1.18. Even then it fell back again. "It depends on the mood of the time but there are times when people have been completely mystified by the strength of the dollar," says Osler. "People find a story that fits the facts but there are so many things going on you can't really explain the full story." Simply put forecasters can have trouble explaining the past, let alone the future.

A game for the masses

While currency trading is for experts, stock trading is for the masses. Huge numbers of ordinary Americans and Asians try their luck in stocks and Europeans, while often more cautious about direct investment, are warming to the idea. Stock markets can be risky and confusing places so investors look to tipsters just as much as punters at the racecourse, at least in the United States. An average European would be hard pressed to name any stock market forecaster but Wall Street is a different matter and has been for a long time. Each generation has produced its market gurus, and none enjoyed greater fame than the bulls who helped to propel the technology boom of the late 1990s, notably Abby Joseph Cohen at Goldman Sachs and Mary Meeker at Morgan Stanley. But a trip back to the 1970s and 1980s reveals one of the better stories of how a guru became immensely influential, only to prove as fallible as the rest of us. His name is Joe Granville.

While currency trading is for experts, stock trading is for the masses.

Self-confidence rather than prescience is what distinguishes Granville. Long before financial TV channels such as CNBC offered stock gurus a stage Granville became famous through his regular commentaries in the "Granville Market Letter," which he sold to thousands of devoted followers. Granville used technical analysis to predict and in the 1970s seemed to have an uncanny knack of spotting markets just as they were turning from boom to bust or vice versa. People believed in him, in fact the whole world seemed to believe him. For instance in January 1981 Granville sent his clients a midnight telegram telling them to "sell everything" and the Dow Jones Industrial Average promptly fell 2.4 percent. Shortly afterwards Granville was confident enough to proclaim: "I'll never make a serious mistake in the market again." So confident was he that he even dabbled in predicting earthquakes. Sadly Granville made enough mistakes – on markets as well as earthquakes – to join Irving Fisher in earning a section of his own in *The Experts Speak*, a 1984 book by Christopher Cerf and Victor Navasky. This work, subtitled *The Definitive Compendium of Authoritative Misinformation*, is a bible for after-dinner speakers and the more honest forecasters who draw on it when admitting the frailties of their work.

In June 1982 the professional pessimist uttered again. "Something is terribly wrong. Sell everything," he said. Disobligingly the Dow began to rise this time but in August Granville dismissed this as "a sucker's rally," predicting it would slump to 450–600 points in 1983. What neither Granville nor anyone else realized at the time was that Dow was breaking out of a range in which it had been stuck since the 1960s. It closed 1983 at 1200 points, double Granville's most optimistic prediction, and off it headed on a bull run which took it past 11,000 in the late 1990s. During this bull run the Dow suffered a brief but spectacular tumble in 1987 which, needless to say, Granville the pessimist failed to predict. But he never gave up and still sends out the newsletter from his base in Kansas City. For a while he even turned bull, saying the Dow would hit 12,000 by the end of 1999. It didn't. Then he turned bear again, forecasting it would plunge to 6000 in the year 2000. It didn't do that, either. But even after the horror of the World Trade Center attacks, he never lost his faith in technical analysis. "I know markets are quick to adjust to the unknown and, while it looks like we are now flying with no parachute, technical analysis thumbs its nose at the terrorists and manages to show us where the supports exist," he said in one of his newsletters.[8] "Terrorism cannot erase the continuity of the market. There will always be a map to follow and its contours will continue to be technically indicated."

Technical analysts such as Granville believe that markets have their own dynamics determined largely by the psychology of investors. But technicians are relatively few compared with fundamentalists. On the stock market fundamentalists try to pin down the future value of shares which, unlike the technicians, they believe is determined largely by the company's future profits. Therefore brokers employ teams of market strategists who predict the overall economic and market environment in which the companies are operating, and analysts who forecast the profits of individual companies. Big brokers issue regular research reports on companies to their clients, usually with three elements:

1 A prediction of the company's earnings per share (EPS) for the coming years. This is a common method for assessing a company's profitability by dividing its net profit by the number of shares it has issued. EPS are commonly expressed in cents or pence.

2 A "target" price which the analyst predicts the company's shares will reach (or fall to). Some analysts calculate the "fair value" of a stock. If the market price goes above fair value the stock is overvalued and not a good buy; if it falls below it is undervalued and may be a good buy.

3 A recommendation of whether to buy, hold or sell the firm's stock.

Analyzing the analysts

Stock recommendations raise the hackles perhaps more than anything else in the equity analysis business. Conflicts of interest at the banks that analyze and sell the same stocks are a major part of this debate. But a later chapter examines this. So for the moment let's assume that stock analysis, forecasting and recommending is honest endeavor untainted by commercial considerations. That still leaves the question: how accurate is it? Share tipping is necessarily subjective and events, dear boy, can throw stock forecasters as much as economists. Nevertheless it would be helpful if they could warn us when a corporation was heading for collapse. Especially if it's the biggest collapse in American history, that of Enron Corporation, an energy group based in Houston, Texas. The Enron scandal initially focused on how its auditors, Andersen, failed to warn shareholders of deals that concealed massive amounts of debt, and links between the company and the politically powerful. But stock analysts also emerge from the affair looking, at best, pretty stupid.

In March 2001 the investment bank Credit Suisse First Boston lowered its 12-month target for Enron. Given what we now know that would seem sensible. But a closer look reveals the figures, in the harsh light of hindsight, to be nonsensical. CSFB cut the target from $128 a share to $110 but that still implied Enron would soar almost 60 percent – the shares were trading at less than $70 at the time – and fly past the record high of $90.56 reached in the euphoric days of August 2000.[9] How wrong can you be? Nine months later Enron collapsed under the weight of its huge debts, filing for bankruptcy protection from its creditors on December 2, 2001. By that time the shares were worth precisely 26 cents on the New York Stock Exchange; in little more than a year Enron's market value had slumped from $80 billion to $220 million. Optimistic forecasts had led many shareholders down the road to financial ruin.

CSFB wasn't alone. Far from warning investors not to touch Enron with a bargepole some analysts recommended buying its stock. A couple of months before the crash, Merrill Lynch, a pillar of Wall Street respectability, upgraded Enron to a "long-term buy."[10] But by the start of November Enron stock had sunk to around $12.50 as the Securities and Exchange Commission, the US markets watchdog, had launched an investigation into its finances. Merrill's analyst, Donato Eassey, lowered his rating on Enron due to uncertainty surrounding the SEC inquiry but only to "neutral." One gets the impression he did so reluctantly. Eassey still didn't recommend selling its stock, announcing to clients that he had "not altered his view of Enron's fundamentals or its ability to weather the long-term storm."[11] Eassey, as they say in these circumstances, no longer works for the company.

Neither of these stories are isolated aberrations. Hard though it is to believe, in early December 2001, 12 of the 17 analysts who covered Enron rated the stock either a hold or buy. The former SEC Chairman Arthur Levitt noted this fact when he testified to a Senate inquiry. "Enron's collapse did not occur in a vacuum. Its backdrop is an obsessive zeal by too many American companies to project greater earnings from year to year," he said. "When I was at the SEC I referred to this as a 'culture of gamesmanship.' A gamesmanship that says it's O.K. to bend the rules, tweak the numbers and let obvious and important discrepancies slide. A gamesmanship where companies bend to the desires and pressures of Wall Street analysts rather than to the reality of numbers. Where analysts more often overlook dubious accounting practices and too often are selling potential investment banking deals."[12]

How do analysts perform in the more humdrum job of forecasting earnings of companies that aren't mired in scandal?

By any standards Enron's demise was an unusual event. So how do analysts perform in the more humdrum job of forecasting earnings of companies that aren't mired in scandal? In London a former financial journalist called Graham Field has created a newsletter service which "analyzes the analysts." Called AQ (Accuracy Quotient) it ranks analysts based on the accuracy of their earnings per share forecasts, with points deducted for revisions. If an analyst makes one forecast, sticks to it, and it proves to be spot on he or she gets a top score of 100. The greater the inaccuracy, the more points are deducted. The same goes for revisions: analysts who change their predictions more often, and by greater amounts than their peers, lose more points. Results are averaged over several years to produce long-term track records. In late 2001 Dutch-Belgian concern Fortis Bank got the top score for continental European coverage of 37 and ABN Amro scored best on British companies with 45. Both scores are a long way from 100.

Field says that in the best cases analysts will come within 1 to 2 percent of predicting the correct EPS, but typically they are 3 to 4 percent adrift. Given all the uncertainties of forecasting stock indices or individual stock prices, these errors are relatively small. That, says Field, is largely because the analysts often have a potential friend in the company investor relations manager. By and large companies want analysts to predict their profits accurately. Corporations don't like analysts getting too optimistic because if the profits fail to meet the forecasts, investors will express their disappointment by selling off their shares. "What everyone wants to avoid in this business is unpleasant surprises," says Field. "An ideal scenario for everyone is an EPS which comes in one or two percent above expectations. Then everyone's happy."[13]

Companies try to steer expectations by employing investor relations staff to keep an eye on the forecasts. If they think a prediction is getting too high they might call the analyst responsible with a few hints to nudge him back in the right direction. "By and large they want to steer the analysts as far as they can towards what they think will be the right number," says Field. This must be done carefully because if the company gives away too much information it risks breaking "fair disclosure" rules. These stipulate that if a company wants to reveal information likely to influence its share price it has to make a public announcement to all investors, large and small.

Companies, which can constantly monitor their sales and costs, naturally have a better idea of how their profits are likely to turn out than outsiders, but still internal predictions go awry sometimes. For instance the British telecom equipment maker Marconi failed for a long time to predict a disastrous collapse in its sales in 2001. So sometimes the friendly man from investor relations doesn't know best, after all. "Companies themselves can have a rather inflated or inaccurate view of where their markets are going," says Field. "In some cases the analyst who's willing to go out on a limb and ignore the advice of investor relations may in fact get things right."

Field, who has compiled league tables of analysts since 1998, says two lessons have emerged. One is that the best-known analysts aren't necessarily the best forecasters. "Some star analysts do carry weight but sometimes if you look more closely at what they're saying their reputation may be greater than their actual forecasting ability," he says. The other conclusion is that few analysts seem to examine their own performance, a culture that the league tables

The best-known analysts aren't necessarily the best forecasters.

seek to challenge. "If you ask an analyst what was their track record they often have no idea," says Field. "There is no culture of accountability. There's no focus on their past record. The focus is on the future."

Notes

1   From "The Record and Improvability of Economic Forecasting," National Bureau of Economic Research Working Paper No 2099, 1986.

2   Interview with author.

3   Interview with author.

4   The analysis was published in Bernstein's newsletter to investors, Economics and Portfolio Strategy, on June 15, 2001.

5   Lehman Brothers Global Foreign Exchange Strategies, by Russell Jones and Giovanni Pillitteri, June 14, 2001.

6   The euro did not start trading until January 1999. For 1997 and 1998 Lehman Brothers used forecasts and actual rates of the German mark against the dollar, and converted them into euros at the official rate of 1.96 marks to the euro set immediately before the currency's launch.

7   The Group of Seven comprises the world's biggest economies: the United States, Japan, Germany, Britain, France, Italy and Canada. Three of them – Germany, France and Italy – have adopted the euro.

8   The Granville Market Letter, October 25, 2001, quoted by Barron's, November 12, 2001.

9   Reported by Reuters March 12, 2001.

10   Reported by Reuters October 9, 2001.

11   Reported by Reuters November 1, 2001.

12   Testifying to the Senate Governmental Affairs Committee, January 24, 2002.

13   Interview with author.

3

The one-handed forecaster

"Give me a one-handed economist! All my economists say, 'on the one hand ... on the other'."

– Harry S. Truman, US President

One of the friction points between economists who work in the hurly-burly of the financial markets and those in universities, central banks or government is the "point forecast." All forecasting involves a risk of being wrong but one way of reducing that risk, and honestly reflecting the uncertainties of real life, is to forecast in ranges. Governments and central banks, keen to secure their reputations for competence with voters and investors, often take this tack because the wider the range, the greater the likelihood their forecast will be right. The European Central Bank might predict inflation in the euro zone will be between 1.1 and 2.1 percent, or Chancellor of the Exchequer Gordon Brown will tell parliament that he expects the British economy to grow between 2.0 and 2.5 percent next year.

Rarely can economists at commercial banks and brokerages get away with such imprecision. Often they serve financial market traders who demand single, pinpoint predictions: the economy will grow 2.2 percent and inflation will be 1.8 percent next year, the euro will be worth 90 US cents a month from now. Period. No ifs, no buts, no "on the one hand this, on the other hand that." In an uncertain world the chances that such precise predictions will be spot on are slim, unless the forecaster is lucky. No doubt many economists serving clients in the markets wish they, too, could spread their safety net widely. But safer forecasts don't necessarily make better forecasts; for instance some economists accuse the European Central Bank of working in such broad ranges as to shed little light on what it really expects. Such hedging of bets can become self-defeating. It's easy to conjure precision from the broadest of ranges peddled by any politician or central banker and this is what happens with the ECB. Economists simply calculate the mid point, or mean average, of its ranges, to produce a point forecast. So if the ECB forecasts inflation of 1.1–2.1 percent, they assume what it really expects is 1.6 percent, bang in the middle. In any case market economists do much the same thing because they deal with uncertainty as much as their colleagues working for the state. Often they, too, come up with a range and then calculate an average figure to satisfy their clients' demand for a point forecast.

Safer forecasts don't necessarily make better forecasts.

Charlie Bean, Chief Economist at the Bank of England, believes that a preoccupation with precision raises public expectations which are impossible to fulfill. It also creates an illusion of certainty that doesn't exist. "One of the consequences of giving point fore-casts is that people think economic forecasters can be precise about the future when we can't," he says. "Many economic fore-casters do the profession a great disservice by concentrating exclusively on what are essentially just mean forecasts."[1] It's important to consider the full range of potential outcomes, not just the one in the middle. Bean, a Cambridge University graduate who once hoped to become a professional cricketer, has little experi-ence of working in commercial banking. His career has alternated between government and the groves of academe. In the second half of the 1970s he worked at the Treasury, rising to coordinate its forecasts during a turbulent time of high inflation, unemployment, and the occasional economic crisis.

In the early 1980s he gained a doctorate from the Massachusetts Institute of Technology, where his thesis was judged by a panel including Robert Solow, a Nobel economics laureate, and a young Lawrence Summers, who later became Treasury Secretary in the Clinton administration. In 1982 Bean joined the London School of Economics where he became a professor before moving to the Bank of England in 2000 as chief econ-omist and one of nine members of its Monetary Policy Committee.

Of course economists don't make forecasts purely for the benefit of market traders.

Of course economists don't make fore-casts purely for the benefit of market traders. Any business wants to have an idea of how the economy will perform in the coming years before making major decisions on investment. There's no point in building a factory, and recruiting staff to run it, if demand for your product has collapsed by the time it opens due to a recession. Long-term investors want an assessment of the risks to their project, not the false certainty of a point forecast which is likely to be wrong. "Economists misrepresent things if they say they expect growth in the US to be 1.7 percent next year and 2.2 the year after that. What's much more useful to the company is to say something about the probabilities either side," says Bean. "Firms often want to know what the extreme events might look like because those are circumstances in which they go broke."

The Bank of England runs an interest rate policy rather than a business, but the needs are similar. So in its quarterly Inflation Report, which despite its name is a broad review of the British economy, the Bank deliberately avoids making point forecasts. There is no single prediction of inflation or GDP. Instead it publishes "fan charts" giving a range of possible outcomes for both indicators (Figures 3.1 and 3.2).

The solid line shows past rates of inflation and GDP growth. Then the forecasts begin, with the darkest band showing the outcome that the Monetary Policy Committee collectively thinks most likely. These charts, published in the Inflation Report of November 2001, show the MPC attaches the greatest probability to inflation being slightly below the 2.5 percent target at the end of 2003 and of GDP growth being above 2.5 percent. The lighter the shade of the band, the less likely the scenario. For example it predicts little likelihood of growth at above 4 percent or below 1 percent. Table 3.1 also gives percentage probabilities of each scenario.[2]

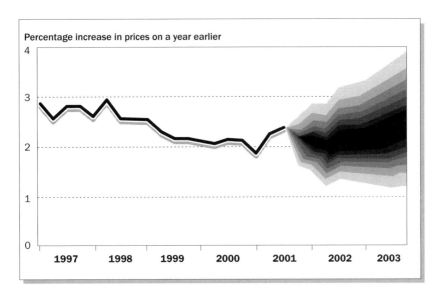

Percentage increase in prices on a year earlier

Figure 3.1 *Fan chart of MPC forecasts of British inflation from the Bank of England Inflation Report, November 2001*

Bean likens this approach to weather forecasters, who might say there's an 80 percent chance of rain tomorrow or a 10 percent chance of a white Christmas. "There's no certainty but they can give you some idea of how likely it is," he says.

"If all the economists were laid end to end they would not reach a conclusion."

Not everyone likes this blurred view of the future; alternative scenarios can provoke the kind of exasperation that made Harry S. Truman demand a one-handed economist, or prompted the Irish playwright George Bernard Shaw to say: "If all the economists were laid end to end they would not reach a conclusion."

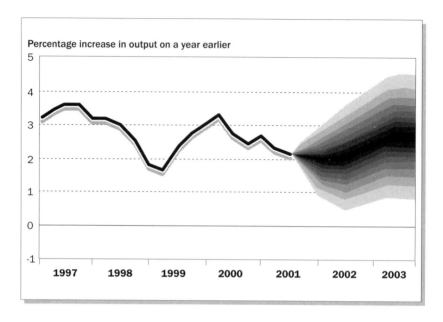

Percentage increase in output on a year earlier

Figure 3.2 *Fan chart of MPC forecasts of British GDP from the Bank of England Inflation Report, November 2001*

Danny Gabay has worked on both sides of the fence. He once wrote economic speeches for former British Deputy Prime Minister Michael Heseltine, a charismatic Conservative who helped to bring down Margaret Thatcher. Gabay later became an economist at the Bank of England, writing the Inflation Report. But in 1999 he switched sides by joining the US investment bank J.P. Morgan. Now he takes the markets' point of view on point forecasts. "Unfortunately we don't live in the world that Charlie Bean does. That's not how the market operates," he says.[3] While economists deal in shades of gray, traders often look

While economists deal in shades of grey, traders often look at the world in black and white.

Bank of England						
Probability	**Range (%)**					
RPIX inflation (4th quarter)	**Less than 1.5**	**1.5–2.0**	**2.0–2.5**	**2.5–3.0**	**3.0–3.5**	**More than 3.5**
2001	1	38	51	9	Less than 1	Less than 1
2002	9	26	32	21	9	3
2003	9	16	24	22	16	13
GDP growth (4th quarter)	**Less than 0**	**0–1**	**1–2**	**2–3**	**3–4**	**More than 4**
2001	Less than 1	Less than 1	39	61	Less than 1	Less than 1
2002	1	9	29	37	19	4
2003	1	6	21	34	27	12

Source: Bank of England Inflation Report, November 2001

Table 3.1 *Bank of England forecasts published in November 2001 for British inflation and economic growth year-on-year, expressed as percentage probablities. The higher the percentage, the greater the probability of the forecast rate being correct, in the Bank's view. For instance, the Bank attached a 51 percent probability to inflation being between 2.0 and 2.5 percent in the fourth quarter of 2001, and a 61 percent probability of the economy growing between 2 and 3 percent in the period. The actual inflation rate was 2 percent but growth fell short of the central forecast at 1.6 percent*

at the world in black and white. Anyone who arrives on a City trading floor – usually raucous and irreverent places – waving a fan chart of probabilities is likely to get a blunt invitation to return when they've made up their mind. "The Bank of England's system is very informative and very useful but it can also be very unhelpful in that the range can be so wide as to encompass all eventualities," says Gabay. "The financial markets, particularly fixed income [bonds], trade on very small margins. There's a big difference between 2.4 percent inflation and 2.6 percent inflation which in the Bank's forecast is completely lost in a fan chart. For us it matters."

BOX 3.1
....

Does thought triumph over the seat of your pants?[1]

Who makes a better forecaster: the thoughtful economist or the seat-of-the-pants trader? Economists and traders may work for the same banks and brokerages but that doesn't mean they always have the same view of the future. For instance in the autumn of 1999 economists predicted British interest rates would hit a peak of 6 percent a year later, but their colleagues on the trading desks felt differently: they bet on 7 percent plus. Who was right?

This time it was the economists. The Bank of England raised its repo rate to 6 percent in February 2000 and left it there for a year. But is it always so? Reuters compared forecasts in its polls of economists with prices on the futures market, where traders bet on interest rates months or even a year or two ahead, and then looked at how rates turned out. Unfortunately the analysis didn't settle disputes long argued over in City trading rooms and bars.

In 2000 the economists beat the market soundly. "When the market does it wrong, it does it in style," said Peter Osler, head of research at futures house GNI. "In 2000 the market got it way off." Traders were way too pessimistic while the economists were spot on. But the economists' record in the late 1990s was not always so good, particularly when a bolt descended from the blue. Probably the biggest such surprise was a Russian economic crisis in the summer of 1998, followed by the near collapse of the LTCM hedge fund. Faced by a threat to the global financial system the US Federal Reserve began slashing rates and the Bank of England followed suit. This caught everyone on the hop, but the economists more so than the markets. In January 1998 economists forecast the repo would be 7.25 percent at the end of the year. It turned out to be a full percentage point lower at 6.25 percent.

Are these comparisons fair? Extrapolating from futures markets is an imprecise science. To get an implied rate you subtract the contract price from 100, so a price of 95 would imply the market expects an interest rate of 5 percent. But futures contracts are based on rates that commercial banks charge each other on three-month loans while the repo is the two-week rate at which the Bank of England lends to the banks. They have different credit risks. As a rule of thumb, three-month interbank rates are a little higher than the repo. But Osler urged caution. "Over a long period of time that is quite a reasonable estimate but it is certainly not always the case."

John Shepperd, an economist at the investment bank Dresdner Kleinwort Benson[2] said economists seemed better at long-term forecasting but otherwise the evidence was inconclusive. "There's surprisingly little (difference) in terms of accuracy," he said. "You may see that as a triumph of the markets over the economists, that people working in markets are just as likely to get it right as economists even though they don't look at the data as closely."

1 This is an edited version of a report published by Reuters on October 24, 2000.
2 The bank has since changed its name to Dresdner Kleinwort Wasserstein.

Investors on some markets are more demanding than others. "Anyone trained in a vaguely academic way to do this subject would recognise there's huge uncertainty in making point forecasts," says Mark Miller, an economist at another US investment bank, Morgan Stanley.[4] "It depends on what area my clients are in. If it's fixed income, there's a definite lust for point forecasts because of the precision of the bond market. For equities you would have a better chance of getting away with a range for a GDP forecast." Share markets, or equity markets as they are also known, tend to be volatile. Especially in the boom years of the 1990s investors were more concerned about rises and falls in the capital value of shares than the level of dividends paid by the company. Bond markets generally move more sedately and the margins of profit or loss are consequently narrower. Precision therefore counts more.

But this still doesn't explain why traders need point forecasts. Why does the difference between 2.4 and 2.6 percent inflation matter? The reason is that markets take bets on economic events. For instance, bonds are sensitive to expectations of inflation. A British government bond may pay nominal annual interest of 5 percent, but that's eroded by inflation of 2 percent, meaning the real interest rate is 3 percent. If inflation rises to 2.5 percent the real interest rate falls, the bond will become less attractive and traders will sell them, depressing their price. If, however, inflation falls the opposite happens: the bond becomes more attractive and its price rises. Traders therefore try to anticipate changes in the inflation rate, which is reported monthly. If they expect inflation to rise, and consequently bond prices to fall, they try to pre-empt this by selling before the figure comes out. Conversely if they expect inflation to fall and bond prices to rise, they'll buy in advance. This is known as taking a position. If a majority of traders on the market takes the same position, the price rise or fall which would have happened after the inflation figure is announced happens beforehand. In the language of the business, the market has "priced in" the expected change in the inflation rate. If the expectations of the majority are fulfilled, bond prices probably won't change when the inflation data flash up on dealers' news screens. But if they've got it wrong traders scramble to buy or sell, depending on whether the rate turned out to be lower or higher than expected, and the market takes a lurch. So only when the data surprise the market – meaning the majority of traders – do prices move significantly. This is when traders make their profits if they play their cards right, and suffer losses if they don't.

The essential ingredient in this game of expectations is the forecast. In fact traders need two forecasts: first their own, according to which they decide what position to take; second the average forecast of all traders, because this determines what the market prices in. Only when the average is determined can anyone know

The essential ingredient in this game of expectations is the forecast.

whether the inflation rate is above, below or in line with expectations when it's released. And it has to be precise. If the market expects inflation to be 2.5 percent, and it turns out to be 2.6, the trader instantly knows that bond prices are likely to fall. So it's not much use knowing there's an 80 percent likelihood that the rate will be somewhere between 2.4 and 2.6 percent. The trader needs to know exactly what his peers expect and this is another argument for point rather than range forecasting.

Every Friday, economists in the City of London (and many other financial centres, for that matter) produce "week ahead" newsletters. These include calendars of key economic data due for release the following week with a forecast of them. News agencies such as Reuters, Bloomberg and Market News collect these and calculate average predictions, which are published as "consensus" forecasts. Consensus suggests that everyone agrees on the prediction but that isn't the case. There's usually a range between the highest and lowest forecast in the sample, say between 2.4 and 2.7 percent for the inflation rate. However, a majority of forecasters tend to cluster near the average so consensus is not an entire misnomer. The range of predictions is itself useful information. If the rate turns out to be a little above or below the consensus forecast, but within the range of expectations, the market reaction may be muted. But if it falls outside the range completely, it's higher or lower than anyone had expected, the reaction may be sharper. These pieces of the expectations jigsaw demand point forecasting: it's much simpler to calculate an average of single figures than of ranges. It's a convention that suits most people in the markets, even if academic economists like Charlie Bean don't like it.

Even commercial bank economists admit the convention has its shortcomings. Economists have a relatively good record in forecasting month to month changes in inflation but other key indicators of the health of the economy such as retail sales data – how much people are spending in the shops – are a more hit and miss affair. Forecasts in Reuters polls confirm this. Over 2001, British economists were on average out by just 0.1 percentage points in forecasting the year-on-year inflation rate (the change in prices between one month and the same month the previous year). In several months they were spot on. By contrast the margin of error for retail sales was six times greater. "One of the ironies of being an economist in the markets is that the better you are, the more insecure you should be. Any economist who believes he has the ability to forecast whether retail sales growth next month will be 0.3 or 0.6 percent is deluding him or herself," says Gabay. "Economics has no useful tools to allow you to do that. The data are too noisy, you're effectively trying to work out how 58 million people interacted with each other on a month-to-month basis. You can't do that."

The better you are, the more insecure you should be.

Nevertheless economists have to set aside their scruples to satisfy the demands of the marketplace. "We are forced to make short term forecasts which we hope are influenced and informed by some kind of basic understanding of the underlying dynamics at play," Gabay says. "But on a month-to-month basis your probability of hitting the number spot on is very low. Numbers can be quite widely wrong ... but that's what gets the market moving." And it's when the market moves that traders make money.

Notes

1 Interview with author.

2 The Bank of England calls the GDP and inflation forecasts "conditional projections" because they are based on unchanged interest rates. Private sector economists usually build assumptions of rate changes into their forecasts.

3 Interview with author.

4 Interview with author.

4

Data watch

"He uses statistics as a drunken man uses lamp posts – for support rather than illumination."

– Andrew Lang, Scottish man of letters[1]

Financial markets live for data. As Danny Gabay said, economic statistics are what gets them moving, particularly when they spring a surprise. Life on the markets is dominated by the calendar of data releases covering many aspects of the economy, domestic or international. Gross domestic product, inflation, employment and unemployment, money supply, retail sales, the number of houses built, the list is almost endless. In a typical week the Reuters diary of US indicators – they're called indicators because they aim to signal how a particular element of the economy is performing – has almost 20 entries. Add the diaries for the wealthy and developing nations together and they list around 130 releases around the world in an average week. Many of them pass almost unnoticed but traders and economists around the world collectively hold their breath before the big indicators appear. Naturally US statistics dominate the agenda. The United States has a $10 trillion economy, equal to one fifth of global GDP,[2] so its fortunes can influence economies and financial markets around the world profoundly.

Economic indicators, like clothing, go in and out of fashion. In times of prosperity attention focuses on the problems that can accompany strong growth, such as inflation. Money supply, the amount of money in circulation and in bank accounts, also becomes popular because sharp increases can herald a rise in inflation. Signs of trouble can mean that the Federal Reserve will push up interest rates to cool things down. However, when the economy hits trouble attention shifts to other indicators. Probably top of the list is the payrolls data which plot the number of jobs created or lost, a timely and sensitive indicator to the state of the American economy, and its stablemate the unemployment rate. Other favorites include retail sales and surveys of consumer confidence. The more confident consumers feel about their personal well being, the more money they are likely to spend. If they fear losing their job, or worse still actually lose it, they cut back spending and a large part of the economy will slow sharply. Naturally, after the shock of September 11, 2001 many economists feared a collapse of consumer confidence but in the event it was a sharp drop in business investment, reacting to the excesses of the technology boom, that pitched America into recession. GDP figures give the broadest picture of the economy but they also take a long time to collect and tend to be outdated when they appear. For instance the first

> **Economic indicators, like clothing, go in and out of fashion.**

estimate of US GDP appears about a month after the quarter (three-month period) on which it reports has ended. So you don't know how the economy performed from January to March until the end of April. A second estimate is released two months after the end of the quarter and this is often heavily revised. GDP figures are based on samples – it would be impossible to record every transaction in the US economy – so in the interests of speed the Department of Commerce rushes out the first estimate based on a relatively small sample. As it processes more information and its sample grows, so it revises the figures if they show a different trend.

Economic indicators emerge from a variety of sources, public and private. Naturally governments play a leading role. While the Department of Commerce handles US GDP, the Department of Labor produces employment and inflation statistics. In the private sector industry groups pitch in. The US Institute for Supply Management produces an index based on a survey of its members which tracks the state of manufacturing industry[3] while the University of Michigan produces the most widely watched survey of consumer confidence. Outside the United States many countries have statistical agencies. In Britain it's simply called National Statistics. The European Union also has an agency called Eurostat, based in Luxembourg, which produces data for the euro zone as a whole, calculating a single inflation rate or single GDP figure for the entire bloc.[4] Central banks also publish closely watched data. For instance the European Central Bank produces money supply figures for the euro bloc while the Bank of Japan's "Tankan" survey of businesses is a key indicator of the world's second biggest national economy.

Most of these bodies publish their data on the internet but this remains a sometimes slow and unreliable system. So most dealers and economists rely on news agencies to report the data rapidly via electronic screens in the trading rooms of banks and brokerages. Biggest among the news agencies are Reuters, a London-based company established more than 150 years ago, and Bloomberg of the United States, which was founded by Michael Bloomberg, now Mayor of New York.

In Britain one of the biggest events of the month is publication of the inflation rate. This figure is significant because the Bank of England uses it as a target. In fact there are many ways of measuring inflation so there's no single rate. However in most countries what matters is retail price inflation, changes in the costs that consumers face in their daily lives. In Britain the main measure is the Retail Price Index which has tracked the cost of living since 1947. Every month National Statistics sends teams around the country to collect the price of everything from a bag of potatoes and a pint of beer to a car and a package holiday in the sun. Altogether about 120,000 prices are collected and fed into a computer program to calculate the index, which tries to mimic the shopping basket of the average British household.

In Britain one of the biggest events of the month is publication of the inflation rate.

But this index is not so much the focus of attention as one of its derivatives known as "RPIX" – the retail price index excluding mortgage interest payments. The standard index includes interest that Britons pay on the mortgage loans they take out to buy their homes. When interest rates rise, so do mortgage repayments and this tends to push up the index. The opposite happens when interest rates fall. But the government and Bank of England prefer a clearer view of inflation which isn't distorted by changes in interest rates that the Bank itself decides. When the Chancellor of the Exchequer, Gordon Brown, handed over control of interest rates to the Bank of England in 1997, he set the Bank a target of keeping annual inflation as close as possible to 2.5 percent on the RPIX index. Rises and falls in the RPIX therefore give traders and economists clues to how the Bank is likely to act. If the annual RPIX rate goes above 2.5 percent the Bank's Monetary Policy Committee may raise interest rates to pull inflation back down, and if it falls significantly below target the bank may cut them. Hence the markets' fascination with RPIX.

A look at the weather

Making short-term forecasts of the RPIX involves some detective work, a lot of number crunching and a look at the weather. The detective work focuses on the components of the index which fluctuate most. "It's a question of breaking up the index, having a look at specific factors like seasonal influences and government measures, putting it all together and coming up with a monthly forecast," says Peter Osler at GNI.[5] Some prices, such as car tax, are set annually but others such as for gasoline are volatile, rising and falling with the world price of oil. So the economist can check with organizations such as the Automobile Association for the average gasoline price, which has a sizeable influence on the index, and calculate how much it has risen or fallen in the past month and in the past year. Another piece in the jigsaw is taxation. For instance, in Britain about

80 percent of the cost of gasoline goes to the government, so any tax changes need to be fed into the forecast. Among the most volatile prices of all are for food, and this is where the weather watch comes in. A wet spell can push the cost of fresh fruit and vegetables up sharply. Mundane though this may seem in the world of high finance, spikes in the cost of potatoes can make the index lurch from month to month. RPIX is not seasonally adjusted, meaning no allowance is made for fluctuations in prices due to the time of year. For example, after Christmas shops traditionally clear surplus stocks by discounting. Therefore the canny forecaster looks back to previous years for signs of seasonal patterns.

Mundane though this may seem in the world of high finance, spikes in the price of potatoes can make the index lurch from month to month.

Once the economist has collected as much price information as possible, the number crunching begins. This is mercifully largely automated using computer spreadsheets based on the shopping basket that National Statistics uses for calculating the index. The spreadsheet throws up an index forecast, and all that remains is to calculate the percentage changes over the previous months and the previous year.

Sometimes quirks in the way inflation data are released give economists a helping hand, particularly in continental Europe. In Germany a number of states such as Bavaria and Lower Saxony issue inflation figures before the national rate appears. Rates in the larger states such as North Rhine–Westphalia, which has a population of 18 million, give strong clues about what the national figure will be. In Italy leading cities issue such comprehensive figures of their own inflation rates that publication later of the national figures tends to a bit of a non-event.

Just as the Bank of England targets RPIX, the European Central Bank aims to keep inflation below 2 percent on the euro zone harmonized index of consumer prices. Much the same rules hold true. If inflation is comfortably below target the ECB might cut interest rates but if it goes well over – such as when it reached a peak of 3.4 percent in May 2001 – the Frankfurt-based bank will be reluctant to lower rates and may even raise them. Once again some pieces of the jigsaw are dropped into the game early. Germany, Italy and France all publish their national inflation rates first so economists can predict fairly accurately what the definitive euro zone figure will be. However, Eurostat has tried to speed up the process since late 2001 by issuing "flash estimates" of euro zone inflation a few days after the month end.

Forecasts piled on forecasts

Economists also look beyond the next release of data to where inflation will be a year or two ahead, or even further into the future. But then they find themselves building ever more assumptions into their calculations so that forecast becomes piled upon forecast. To project where inflation will be in a couple of years' time the economist may have to predict economic growth even further ahead. According to orthodox economics the inflation cycle lags the economic cycle. Higher GDP growth can provoke higher inflation because demand for goods and services rises at times of prosperity faster than the economy can satisfy it. But usually inflation doesn't start rising until a while after growth has accelerated. When growth slows inflation tends to follow suit, again at a respectful distance. A key part of the calculation is predicting the "output gap." That's the difference between the economy's capacity to produce goods and services, and demand for them. Inflation is unlikely to cause problems if the economy is working below full capacity because of slack demand. During recessions consumers put off buying a new car so manufacturers offer discounts to clear the rows of unsold vehicles. In boom times the output gap vanishes: demand outstrips the economy's capacity to meet it and inflation picks up. The car maker will raise prices if its factory is working flat out and still the orders flood in.

Generally the task of central banks is to smooth out the peaks and troughs of the economic cycle and keep inflation in check by raising and lowering interest rates. That creates its own problems for the prediction business. For instance, when the Bank of England or European Central Bank forecast growth and inflation, they assume unchanged interest rates; otherwise they would end up predicting their own decisions.[6] But in the real world central banks rarely leave rates unchanged for more than a few months. In the past decade only in one year, 1993, did the Federal Reserve not change its fed funds target. By contrast, in 1991 it cut the rate 10 times and in 2001 no fewer than 11 times. Thus an economist ends up making an inflation forecast which is based on a GDP forecast which in turn is based on an interest rate forecast. "The further you go out [into the future] the bigger your likely error," says Osler.

The task of central banks is to smooth out the peaks and troughs of the economic cycle and keep inflation in check by raising and lowering interest rates.

Given that the further into the future you peer, the greater the uncertainties, many economists making GDP predictions more than two years ahead revert to using the "trend" rate of growth. This is the average growth rate calculated over several decades. Economists argue over the niceties of what constitutes trend growth but for example between 1970 and 2000 US GDP grew on average 3.1 percent a year, Japan's 3.8 percent, Germany's 2.4 percent and Britain's 2.3 percent. This concept is rooted in the phenomenon of "regression to the mean," which the Victorian statistician Francis Galton discovered not in economics but in nature.

BOX 4.1
....

Man and machine

Some forecasts emerge not from man but machine. Computer programs which try to model the real economy are widely used in forecasting, although humans rarely resist the temptation to tweak what emerges from them. Known as econometric models they use networks of equations which mimic linkages in the economy by calculating what effect a change in one variable has on others. For instance if economic growth accelerates inflation is likely to follow suit, and central banks will react by raising interest rates. When interest rates rise, the economy is likely to slow and inflation will fall. These webs are set out in large computer spreadsheets. If the economist changes a forecast of interest rates, the spreadsheet automatically recalculates forecasts of inflation, GDP and so on. In the 1970s and 1980s models became ever larger and more complex, with hundreds of equations, but recently simplicity has become fashionable.

Trevor Williams, an economist at the British bank Lloyds TSB, uses conventional methods to forecast up to a year ahead but then he

---

boots up the model. "They're not good at forecasting short-term turning points but they do particularly well on longer-term forecasting," he says. "They're better at scenario planning, that is to say 'if this event happened, what would be the likely outcome?'." For instance if the government announces changes in spending and taxation the model predicts the likely effect on the economy. But econometric models suffer from the pitfall that bedevils all forecasting techniques: the past is not always a reliable guide to the future. Equations in the models are based on past experience but economies evolve. For instance in the 1970s and 1980s average earnings of Britons accelerated whenever unemployment fell but that link weakened in the 1990s due to reforms which meant that a low jobless rate didn't automatically create a labor shortage. At first the models missed this change in the structure of the British economy and consequently they overestimated wage growth and inflation as unemployment fell. The Treasury and Bank of England use econometric models and their weaknesses may have contributed to the caution which Ken Clarke complains about in Chapter 2. Clarke made his feelings clear to his officials. "They were completely obsessed with economic modelling," he says. "The whole approach to the budget began with the presentation of the forecast based on the Treasury model. They constantly urged me to make this the basis of the budget judgment ... and of monetary policy decisions. Of course it was very, very unreliable. The model was consistently too pessimistic and at odds with one's feel for the real economy." So which decided the budget forecasts: the Treasury model or Ken Clarke's feel for the real economy? "They were a combination of the two," he says. "We used to argue them over and eventually we would settle at a figure."

Galton discovered that children of exceptionally tall or short parents "regressed" to the average height of the population. Tall parents tend to have tall children but not usually as tall as they are. Short parents tend to have short children but not usually as short as they are. This doesn't always hold true but children tend to have heights closer to the mean than their parents. The phenomenon applies equally to economies. If GDP grows well above the long-term average in one period, you should forecast that economic perform-ance thereafter will be less outstanding. Over time the growth rate will return towards the average.

However, just as not all people are average height, economies reg-ularly over- or undershoot the long-term average. In the past three decades only in one year, 1970, did the British economy grow at its average rate of 2.3 percent (although in a couple of years it came close at 2.4 percent). Admittedly the British economy has undergone wilder swings than many of its peers in the wealthy world, ranging from a mighty 7.4 percent growth in 1973 to a ghastly contraction of 2.2 percent in 1980.

According to orthodox thought, an economy is in balance when GDP grows near the trend rate. If growth goes too far above for too long the risk is that supply will not keep pace with demand, stoking the fires of inflation. That forces the central bank to raise interest rates and slow the economy enough to bring supply and demand back into balance. Politicians, particularly in

For sustainable growth read trend growth.

Britain which has suffered more than its fair share of booms and busts, like to talk of "sustainable growth" – a happy state where the economy steadily expands at an unspectacular rate, and keeps doing so year in, year out. For sustainable growth read trend growth.

New Economy?

Any mention of trend growth is likely to arouse one of the great arguments among economists, and the biggest headaches for forecasters of recent times: whether the United States and Britain to a lesser extent have a "New Economy." Definitions of the New Economy differ wildly from extreme enthusiasts who believed the United States could wave goodbye to recessions, to a more cautious majority who thought it could at least enjoy longer periods of stronger growth, punctuated by fewer, shorter recessions. At the heart of the debate lay a puzzle: as US growth accelerated in the mid-1990s there was no sign of its usual companion – rising inflation. For most of the decade inflation remained meekly at 3 percent or less, while GDP growth reached annual rates of over 6 percent in some quarters. In the second half of the 1990s growth averaged 4.1 percent, well above the long-term average of 3.1 percent. The effect on Americans' wealth was tremendous. In 2000, the US economy produced $2.5 trillion more than it had in 1991, meaning it had grown 38 percent in a decade even when adjusted for inflation.

Economists searched round for an explanation of this inflation-free growth and came up with the New Economy. An explosion in technology use, particularly computing systems and telecommunications, had made the American economy more productive. Added to this was greater global competition due to deregulation, which kept down prices even as demand rose, and a more flexible labor force, meaning that unemployment could fall steadily without creating shortages of workers which push up pay and prices. Unquestionably all this was happening in the United States but a big question remained: was this a temporary phenomenon that would vanish at the next downturn, or was it a change in the very structure of the US economy that would last indefinitely?

Not even Alan Greenspan, the Fed Chairman, was sure. "We do not now know, nor do I suspect can anyone know, whether current developments are part of a once or twice in a century phenomenon that will carry productivity trends nationally and globally to a new higher track, or whether we are merely observing some unusual variations within the context of an otherwise generally conventional business cycle expansion," he said on July 22, 1997. "The recent improvement in productivity could be just transitory, an artifact of a temporary surge in demand and output growth." One thing was certain, however: this quandary played havoc with Fed forecasts. In the same testimony to Congress he reported that Fed policymakers expected GDP to grow 3 to 3.25 percent that year and a cooler 2 to 2.5 percent in 1998. They were way too pessimistic: it actually grew 4.4 percent in 1997 and 4.3 percent in 1998.

As the years went by and the economy kept booming, Greenspan warmed to the idea of a New Economy and even let the term slip into his testimony. Back at Congress in February 2000 he said: "It is certainly true that we have a new economy. It is different. It is behaving differently and it requires a different type of monetary policy to maintain its stability and growth than we had in the past."[7] Later that year Greenspan also showed willingness to slaughter a sacred cow of forecasters and monetary policymakers alike, the "non-accelerating inflation rate of unemployment," known as the NAIRU. According to this theory if unemployment falls below a given level the pool of available workers becomes so small that employers have trouble finding people to fill vacancies. Labor shortages push up wage costs which employers pass on to their customers and inflation starts climbing. Unemployment below the NAIRU had been a useful signal of inflation on the way but in 2000 the jobless rate was only 4 percent and inflation remained tame. So was it a handy signal any more? Greenspan thought not. "My forecast is that the NAIRU which served as a very useful statistical procedure to evaluate how the economy was behaving over a number of years, like so many types of temporary models which worked, is probably going to fail in the years ahead as a useful indicator," he said.

Of course it all came to an abrupt end along with the boom in 2001. That year 2.6 million Americans lost their jobs, unemployment bounced back to 5.8 percent and a recession began. Nevertheless, well into the recession Greenspan remained a believer in the New Economy. In January 2002 he said that technology might change the shape and length of downturns for the better because businesses had more timely information on their markets and could therefore sort themselves out more quickly. "Contractions initially may be steeper, but because imbalances are more readily contained, cyclical episodes overall should be less severe than would be the case otherwise," he said.[8]

Ken Clarke's hunch

Real or imagined, the New Economy seems to have passed the rest of the world by.

Real or imagined, the New Economy seems to have passed the rest of the world by. While America boomed, Japan drifted in and out of recession, having lost its touch for high growth that was so evident until the end of the 1980s. Continental Europe fared better but was unable to shift into a higher gear, perhaps due to a lot of red tape which kept unemployment close to 10 percent. But was Britain, which radically deregulated its economy in the 1980s and 1990s, an exception? Ken Clarke thought he spotted some New Economy elements while he ran the Treasury in the 1990s, but it led him into more disputes with the Bank of England. "I thought the potential for inflation had been reduced by a level of intensity of global competition which we had not known in the 1980s ... We were also going through a period of very rapid techno-logical change which enabled people to respond to any labour constraints more rapidly," he says. "My hunch was that the British economy could sustain growth at more than 2.5 percent without inflation and I was cautiously testing that theory. I thought that somewhere between 2.5 and 3 percent in modern circumstances could probably be sustained without any serious risk of inflation."[9]

This is why, says Clarke, he refused to raise interest rates before the 1997 election. At the time cynics accused him of sitting on his hands because a rate rise would kill any hope that his Conservative government had of survival. Clarke dismisses the very thought but admits that he disagreed with the Governor of the Bank of England, Eddie George, on how much growth the economy could sustain. Under the rules of the day the final decision on rates lay with the Chancellor so Clarke had his way for a while.

But after the election came a new government and a new system. Labour despatched Clarke and the Conservatives from office and the new Chancellor, Gordon Brown, immediately raised interest rates. Then he handed control of monetary policy to the Bank, which raised rates another five times in the following 12 months. When Clarke left the Treasury the official rate had been 6 percent; by the middle of the following year it was 7.5. Unbowed, Clarke points out that the economy came close to stalling in early 1999. The Bank of England, he says, forced rates too high because of that bugbear of British monetary policy, bad forecasts. "Subsequent events vindicated me. The one thing the Bank of England couldn't forecast, which was demonstrated to me over and over again, was inflation," he says. "If you look back over the history of disagreements over interest rates it's quite obvious that I was quite right and Eddie was wrong. Eddie's rapid increase in interest rates after the election was plainly wrong."

Over at the Bank's headquarters on Threadneedle Street, Chief Economist Charlie Bean is cautious about any New Economy effect. But he admits the Bank's forecasts hadn't been spot on and this might signal something stirring in the British economy. "One of the features of forecasting in recent years has been to under predict growth a little bit and over predict inflation. We're not alone in that. Most forecasters have made that same mistake," he says. "That's a sign that something good has happened on the supply side but tracking exactly what is not as easy as you might think ... My personal view is that there's something in the new economy explanation of the rise in productivity in the US," he says. "I'm cautiously optimistic that we may see some sort of productivity acceleration in the UK although so far it has not really been evident in the data. Productivity performance has not been very good here."[10]

Sushil Wadhwani, a former member of the Bank's Monetary Policy Committee, has quantified the forecasting error made by City economists. Between 1993 and 1999 GDP growth was almost 0.5 percentage points higher than the average forecast while inflation was slightly more than 0.5 percent below the predicted rate. These may seem small but in economic terms there's a big difference between 2.4 percent growth, as forecast by the City pundits, and 2.9 percent as it turned out. "Virtually all forecasters (including the Bank of England) failed to spot the improvement in the growth-inflation trade off during the 1990s," he said.[11] Wadhwani was an enthusiastic supporter of the New Economy concept on the Committee, and was consistently dovish on interest rates, believing they could be kept relatively low without provoking inflation. Nevertheless, he issued a warning. "Although it is easy to be excited by the structural changes that are happening, it is impor-tant to emphasise that while the 'New Economy' considerations ... have important disinflationary effects, they do not imply the death of inflation." Governor George made a nod towards Wadhwani but remained skeptical. "Some people are more persuaded by this than others," he said. "We keep an open mind but aren't yet ready to bet the ranch on it."[12]

Clarke, on the other hand, admires Greenspan for pushing growth to its limits and ignoring the Cassandras. "I think Alan Greenspan is one of the shrewdest, cleverest men I've ever met," he says. "If Alan Greenspan had followed all the conventional advice he was given, if he had been tied to this traditional forecast, he would have tightened policy in the mid 1990s and would have killed off American growth."

Notes

1 Alan L. Mackay *Harvest of a Quiet Eye*; attributed this quote to Andrew Lang.

2 This is calculated according to purchasing power parity, a system of converting currencies which eliminates price differences between countries. Using market exchange rates US GDP accounts for a third of global GDP in dollar terms.

3 The ISM also produces a non-manufacturing survey of services industry activity. The ISM is better known by its former name of the National Association of Purchasing Managers (NAPM).

4 Eurostat collates data provided by national statistical agencies of the 12 euro zone nations. The European Central Bank monitors these overall figures when deciding interest rates. Eurostat also produces indicators for the entire European Union but these are of less interest because the three states outside the euro zone – Britain, Sweden and Denmark – have their own currencies and interest rates.

5 Interview with author.

6 The Reserve Bank of New Zealand, widely acknowledged to be the most transparent central bank in the world, does predict its own interest rate decisions. However these forecasts frequently turn out to be as wrong as anybody else's.

7 Testimony before Senate Banking Committee, February 23, 2000.

8 Speech to Bay Area Council, San Francisco, January 13, 2002.

9 Interview with author.

10 Interview with author.

11 Speech on October 12, 2000.

12 Testifying to parliamentary committee, November 22, 2000.

5

Recession watch

"Whatever disaster occurs, the same disaster isn't likely to occur twice. Whatever brings on the next recession, it will not resemble the last recession."
– Kenneth Clarke, British Chancellor of the Exchequer 1993–1997

Recessions are rare events and usually don't last very long; at least this is the record of most wealthy nations since World War Two. That's a relief because, as Alan Greenspan discovered in 1990, they tend to creep up unnoticed on policymakers and forecasters alike. "In the UK and the US the experience is that we have to be pretty well into the recession year before everybody owns up and says things are bad," says Roy Batchelor, professor of banking and finance at the City University Business School in London. "It's sad but true. At the times when you most need [forecasts] they're rather fragile ... We're really bad at seeing the minus numbers coming."[1]

Definitions of what constitutes a recession vary. On financial markets it usually means two successive quarters, or six months, in which GDP shrank but some economists believe the economy has to contract over a whole calendar year to qualify. In the United States the accepted arbiter of recessions is the National Bureau of Economic Research, an independent organization based in Cambridge, Massachusetts. The NBER uses a complex formula to determine recessions, the start and end of which are declared by its Business Cycle Dating Committee, a group of six leading academic economists. They study a variety of monthly indicators, including unemployment, personal income, industrial production and sales by companies in the manufacturing and trade sectors of the economy. But the committee puts little weight on the GDP figures because they are published only quarterly and often revised substantially. Usually it takes time for recessions to show up in the figures and the six wise men don't like to be hurried into declaring the peaks and troughs of the American economy. For instance they waited until late November 2001 before announcing the country had gone into recession the previous March.

Definitions of what constitutes a recession vary.

As a rule industrial economies grow far more than they shrink, otherwise everyone would be no better off than 50 or 100 years ago. According to the NBER the US had nine recessions between the end of World War Two and the latest downturn, but they lasted on average only 11 months each. They added up to less than nine of the 56 years between 1945 and 2001. America's longest period of unbroken growth was its most recent, which lasted 10 years from March 1991.[2] Naturally the pre-war record is worse thanks to the

Great Depression, when the US economy contracted from August 1929 – a couple of months before the stock market collapsed – to March 1933. That bumped up the average US recession between the end of the first and second wars to 18 months. The Depression cannot be compared with anything that has happened since. Between 1929 and 1933 the economy contracted by more than a quarter – it shrank 13 percent in 1932 alone – and one in four American workers had no job. By contrast the worst recession year in the past half century was 1982 when GDP fell two percent and unemployment peaked with one in 10 out of a job. Of course not all modern-day recessions are as shallow or short lived, particularly outside the club of wealthy nations. Apart from Indonesia's nightmare in 1998 Argentina endured four years of recession and 20 percent unemployment before its economy collapsed at the end of 2001. Worse still Russia suffered something akin to the Great Depression in the 1990s after the break up of the Soviet Union. Following the collapse of Communism the Russian economy contracted at annual rates of up to 18.6 percent for seven years until it finally began growing in 1999.[3]

The problem with predicting recessions is that they come in different shapes and sizes, and attack from different angles. "One of my layman's theories on economic policy is that whatever disaster occurs, the same disaster isn't likely to occur twice. Whatever brings on the next recession, it will not resemble the last recession,"[4] says Ken Clarke who, in conspicuous contrast to some of his Conservative predecessors, managed to complete his term as Chancellor without a recession. Nevertheless his rule of thumb holds. Economic expansions tend to succumb to one or more of three maladies: a financial crash, an overheated economy, or an external shock.

The hangover that follows the party

With the exception of those provoked by external shocks, recessions are usually the hangover that follows the party. They're nature's way of purging excess. When the likes of Greenspan speak of "correcting imbalances in the economy" what they really mean is cleansing the sins of overindulgence.

> With the exception of those provoked by external shocks, recessions are usually the hangover that follows the party.

The American boom of the late 1990s succumbed to at least two, if not all three maladies: a stock market crash which wiped out trillions of dollars in paper wealth plus excessive investment in fashionable high technology business ventures, much of which was financed by debt. If that wasn't enough to tip the economy over the cliff then the September 11 attacks completed the process.

In many countries the stock market is a game for a small group of wealthy people, but not in the United States. By 2001 almost half of US households owned shares through mutual funds (unit trusts). Their wealth tied up in stocks rocketed from $4.5 trillion in 1994 to more than $14 trillion in early 2000. That was equal to almost $50,000 for every American. They got used to feeling rich and went on a spending spree, often financed not by selling the shares but by their credit cards. Then the bubble burst; just as bull markets create wealth, bear markets destroy it. The tumble in stock prices in the year after the March 2000 peak wiped out $2 trillion in Americans' paper wealth. The "feel good" factor evaporated. Some recessions follow when consumers curb their spending, as they did in the United States in 1990.

But in 2001 it was corporate America which led the way down. During the technology boom business also got carried away. Investment is a great thing provided it produces a return, but in bubble economies everyone becomes overoptimistic. People buy shares at inflated prices, believing they will keep rising, and companies sink large sums into investments with slim chances of producing a profit. Excessive optimism is common at times of technological advance. It happened in the railway age – many of the lines built never made money – and it has happened in the internet age. Every corporation seemed to produce an internet strategy but how many made any money out of it? Money poured down the drain in copious amounts. A similar bout of overoptimism, overinvestment and overborrowing also helped to plunge many East Asian nations into crisis in 1997–1998. Whether in Silicon Valley or in Seoul, when businesses woke up to reality they stopped investing and tried to cut their debt. Those that couldn't failed.

As ever, the recessions that followed purged these excesses the hard way. Having missed the boat in 1990 Greenspan was clearly anxious not to do so again and he began worrying aloud that the American boom might end in tears as early as December 5, 1996. That's when he warned US investors against "irrational exuberance." Few people wanted to listen. The Dow Jones Industrial Average fell the next day to 6382 points but it was to rise more than 5000 points in the following four years before finally responding to Greenspan's medicine. The intervention remained verbal until June 1999 but then the Fed began raising interest rates to stop the economy overheating. Overheating has been the most common culprit in provoking recent recessions in the West. Monetary authorities push up interest rates to subdue inflation but, in doing so, kill off economic growth. It's not only a US phenomenon: Nigel Lawson led Britain into a classic boom and bust cycle in the late 1980s.

Stock market bubbles, and booms and busts are largely home grown, but the external shock is, by definition, an event over which policymakers, be they in government or central banks, have little or no control. A tripling of the oil price in the 1970s, engineered by the OPEC cartel of crude exporters, helped to trigger recessions around the world although policymakers made a bad situation worse by raising interest rates to tackle inflation provoked by the oil shock. The Iraqi invasion of Kuwait was a leading factor in the US downturn of 1990–1991. We now know the United States had been in recession for six months when four airliners slammed into the World Trade Center, the Pentagon and a Pennsylvanian field on September 11. But that doesn't mean this most shocking of external shocks didn't play its part. "Before the attacks it is possible that the decline in the economy would have been too mild to qualify as a recession. The attacks clearly deepened the contraction and may have been a factor in turning the episode into a recession," said economists at the NBER in a memo.[5]

> **Stock market bubbles, and booms and busts are largely home grown, but the external shock is an event over which policymakers have little or no control.**

Soul searching

Given the gravity of recessions, it's not surprising that the record of economists in foreseeing them comes under scrutiny and any failures provoke soul searching. Prakash Loungani, an economist at the International Monetary Fund in Washington, has studied the strike rate as part of his research into the overall accuracy of economics forecasts.[6] Sadly this academic work corroborates the anecdotal evidence on recession watching. Loungani, who worked for the Federal Reserve in Chicago and at its Washington headquarters before joining the IMF, has analyzed a decade of forecasts made between October 1989 and December 1999 on 63 countries ranging from the United States, which had one downturn in the period and the Netherlands which had none, to Ukraine which spent the entire decade in recession. Loungani defined a recession as a year in which GDP fell in real terms (after adjusting for inflation). To the list of recessions he adds a further type, the kind suffered by Russia and Ukraine, and to a less painful extent by former Soviet satellites such as Poland and Hungary. These are contractions when countries dismantled their systems of central planning and replaced them with market economies.

Loungani analyzed figures produced by Consensus Economics, a London-based company which collects predictions from economists, calculates averages and sells the data back to the markets. It began publishing figures for the leading industrial nations in October 1989 and gradually expanded the service to include developing nations in Latin America, Asia and post-Communist Europe by 1995. In the sample there were 72 recessions and the results are sobering for the forecasting profession (Table 5.1).

Forecasts of recessions

	Month	Number of recessions forecast out of 72	Number of GDP forecasts higher than outcome
Year before recession	February	2	60
	April	2	60
	June	2	56
	August	2	56
	October	4	56
	December	8	60
Year of recession	February	23	63
	April	26	61
	June	35	59
	August	41	54
	October	50	50
	December	54	40

Source: IMF

Table 5.1 *Recession forecasting: the record*

Loungani found that in the August preceding the recession year forecasters had predicted just two of the downturns. By December – only a month before the recession year began – the figure had risen but remained less than dazzling, just eight of the 72 recessions in the study. Thereafter economists gradually cottoned on but oh so slowly. By April two-thirds of the recessions remained undetected and in June more than half of them had yet to be predicted. Even as the years drew to a close in December the economists had yet to recognize a quarter of the recessions, even though it wasn't so much a case of forecasting any more as spotting contractions which were already underway. Another disturbing finding is that even when the economists spotted a recession they failed to realize how deep it would be. Even in the December of the recession year, well over half the forecasts – 40 out of the 72 – proved to be overoptimistic, in other words they underestimated the size of the contraction.

Snapshot of the past

How can so many economists, from Alan Greenspan downwards, fail so often to realize recessions are going on around them? The answer lies in the raw materials of forecasting: statistics. Economic indicators are largely a snapshot of the past, not the present, let alone the future. Even in the most sophisticated economies it takes time to collect, process and publish data on how they are performing. Economists have to predict, the future using figures which are out of date the day they're published. Spare a thought for anyone following, yet alone trying to predict, the euro zone economy. To find out how GDP fared in a given quarter they have to wait more than two months after it has ended before Eurostat releases its first estimate, and three and a half months for the second, more considered estimate. For instance the second estimate of GDP in the third quarter of 2001, which ended in September, was published on January 10 the following year. That's not so much news as recent history. The US Commerce Department gets its GDP figures out more quickly but it still takes a month after the quarter has ended. And there's a price to pay: in statistics there's a trade-off between speed and accuracy. Fast data tends to be inaccurate data that needs big revisions. For instance the first time GDP data signalled that America might be heading into its latest recession was at the end of October 31, 2001 when the Commerce Department published its first estimate for the third quarter (July–September). This showed GDP shrank at a modest annual rate of 0.4 percent. But

How can so many economists fail so often to realize recessions are going on around them?

the figure flattered to deceive: a month later the Department revised it to –1.1 percent and on December 21 it issued a third estimate showing the economy had contracted 1.3 percent. So in less than a couple of months the downturn worsened by almost one percentage point. One percent of a $10 trillion economy is $100 billion, more than the entire GDP of Egypt in the year 2000. Yet still the data didn't signal a recession because the economy has to shrink in *two successive* quarters to qualify. Everyone awaited GDP figures for the last quarter of 2001, confident they would confirm the downturn had begun. But never underestimate the power of statistics to surprise: at the end of January the first release showed that the economy had *expanded*, although only 0.2 percent. Subsequently the growth figure was revised to a more robust 1.7 per cent. So 10 months after America went into recession, according to the wise men of the NBER, the Commerce Department statistics had yet to confirm this. By early 2002 it all started to look a bit academic; many economists believed the recession was almost over and were busy forecasting the recovery.

If you're confused by these seemingly contradictory figures delivered months after the event, spare a thought for Alan Greenspan who has to set the interest rates. This confusion isn't unique to the latest recession so it's hardly surprising that he had trouble spotting the last one in 1990. Naturally the Fed can't sit around waiting for official GDP data before acting; given the time lag it would permanently miss the boat. The art of good central banking is to anticipate rather than react. Some statistics have a better record in signalling the future. For instance, fluctuations in the level of new orders that businesses receive indicate

The art of good central banking is to anticipate rather than react.

fairly reliably how much they will produce later on. Such forward-looking figures are known as leading indicators, as opposed to lagging indicators. Greenspan and his fellow policymakers at the Fed sift vast amounts of this kind of data for a picture of the future.

A chastened Greenspan?

So did Greenspan anticipate the recession of 2001, the second in his career as Fed chief? Undoubtedly he was much faster off the mark, perhaps chastened by the experience of 1990. "Certainly he was wrong in the last recession. That probably prompted him to be particularly energetic and quick in this one. He certainly learnt from this process," says business cycle expert Victor Zarnowitz.[7] The Fed began cutting interest rates on January 3, 2001, more than two months before the recession started. But while financial markets can react instantly to interest rate changes the overall economy moves much more slowly: it can take two or even three years to absorb them fully. So while Greenspan anticipated the 2001 recession the Fed acted too late to avert it, insofar as central banks can prevent downturns. All he could do was try to keep it as short and as shallow as possible. And given that downturns span anything from a half percent contraction lasting a year, to double digits lasting several years, even anticipating relatively late in the day is worthwhile. The alternative can be calamitous. For four years the US government made the Depression incalculably worse by refusing to stimulate the economy. Only when Franklin D. Roosevelt launched his "New Deal" in 1933 did America start to recover.

The state holds no monopoly on economic data and private organizations often try to plug gaps in the official figures. Some have overcome the time lag problem by surveying relatively small numbers of well-informed people, asking a few, straightforward questions so that the results can be published rapidly. An example is purchasing managers' indices, the oldest of which is compiled monthly by the US Institute for Supply Management (ISM). More recently the model has been applied to Europe in a series of indices sponsored by Reuters. The format is simple. For the euro zone index 2500 manufacturing companies in eight countries are asked whether various aspects of their business, such as output, new orders and employment levels, have risen, fallen or stayed the same in the past month. From their answers indices are compiled on which 50 marks the no change level. Any figure above 50 signals expansion and any figure below contraction. In a business where speed is of the essence they score top marks. The indices usually appear on the first working day after the month has ended, a far cry from the long waits for official figures. They can also serve forecasters as valuable early warning devices. For instance the US ISM Index fell below 50 in August 2000, a good year before the recession in the overall economy showed up in official figures. But the results need careful interpretation. Manufacturing accounts for only one-fifth of US GDP and it's possible for the sector to suffer its own recession without the rest of the economy following suit.

So why not conduct similar surveys in the services sector, which contributes almost two-thirds of output in the wealthy nations? That's precisely what happens but it's notoriously difficult to measure the services economy. A car maker can easily report whether it has made more or fewer vehicles in the past month but how does a hospital or a law firm measure its "output?" Also the services indices are relatively new and economists like to check their track record over a decade or two of expansions and downturns before trusting them fully. Surveys don't just quiz captains of industry: some cover groups such as consumers, the ordinary shoppers on the street. Consumer spending accounts for two-thirds of demand in the wealthy nations so their moods are key to whether an economy grows or contracts. After the September 11 attacks, the crucial question was whether or not Americans would stay at home and cut back their spending, deepening the recession which we now know was already underway. Hence the exhortations from politicians to go out and spend.

Surveys aren't perfect any more than the official figures are. Again there can be a trade off between speed and accuracy. For instance, the Confederation of British Industry produces a survey of its members, which include the country's biggest corporations, and the results are generally a reliable indicator of economic trends. But generally doesn't mean always. In late 1998 the CBI survey signalled that Britain was heading into a recession in 1999 which never materialized.

Revisions to official figures are not unique to the United States; they're a big headache for forecasters around the world. According to Richard Jeffrey, an economist formerly at Charterhouse Economics in London, initial estimates of British GDP were revised up by an average 0.5 percentage points between 1992 and 2000. Looking at figures published quarterly Jeffrey found that on six occasions the growth rate was revised up by one percent or more. This may not sound much but an economy growing 1.5 percent a year is weak, one growing 2.5 percent a year is robust. Sometimes revisions can even

Revisions to official figures are not unique to the United States; they're a big headache for forecasters around the world.

turn recession into growth. Initially National Statistics reported that the British economy shrank 0.5 percent in 1992. Yet six years after the event it changed the way of calculating GDP, turning 1992 into a year of growth, albeit a tiny 0.1 percent. "In no particular order statisticians are faced by incomplete data, inaccurate data, changing seasonal variations in activity, and a changing industrial structure. All these can cause disruption, often resulting in errors compounding one another," said Jeffrey.[8]

A record of inaccuracy

Paul Ormerod, a London-based economist, has even suggested that economic statistics can be so inaccurate as to make forecasting a hopeless task. The problem lies in "noise," random movements that bedevil statistics and hide underlying trends. "The fact is that macroeconomic data series are dominated by noise and contain little genuine information," he said. "In general all growth rate forecasts are likely over time to give errors that are similar in size to the variable that is being forecast. The clear implication is that, in the current state of scientific knowledge, it is simply not possible to improve on the existing record of forecasting accuracy – or inaccuracy, which might be a more appropriate description. This conclusion holds regardless of the particular economic theory or statistical technique used."[9] Ormerod has written a number of books expounding his theories, one of which is appropriately called The Death of Economics.

At the IMF Loungani also offers a couple of explanations for the forecasters' poor record. One is the "noise" problem. Economists are loath to change their predictions when one, or even a few indicators suggest the business cycle is close to a turning point. A graph of an economy rarely moves in smooth upward and downward lines.

Inevitably it bounces around, having some weaker quarters in an upswing and some stronger quarters in a downturn. Whereas financial markets will nervously react to isolated indicators, economists must distinguish the noise from the trend, so they await corroborative data. This brings about a "recognition lag" which appears not only at the start of recessions but also at the end of them. Economists make better "recovery watchers" than recession watchers but only if downturns fall in line with the average length, which since World War Two has been less than a year in the United States. "A few recessions do end up lasting longer: when that happens, the evidence suggests that forecasters are caught flat-footed," said Loungani.[10] Caution remains the watchword for economists. "They are slow in getting pessimistic but once they get pessimistic they are slow in calling the recovery. The lag before the forecasters recognise the recovery is typically about three months," he says. "In fairness to them the first month or two of recovery is a fairly dicey time. You are worried about a false bottom. It could just be bouncing along the bottom rather than having a true recovery. But in a sense that is what forecasters are paid to tell you."[11]

The Cassandra effect

Perhaps Greek mythology, in the form of the beautiful but accursed Cassandra, can explain why forecasters fail to foresee recessions. In one version of the story Cassandra refused to make love with Apollo unless he gave her the gift of prophecy. Apollo obliged but still she rejected his advances, so the sun-god retaliated with a curse that no one would ever believe her. In vain Cassandra predicted the sack of Troy and her own murder but the curse of Apollo remained with her to the end.

In 1999 Victor Zarnowitz fell victim to what might be called the "Cassandra effect," albeit in less dramatic circumstances. That spring he published an article in the *Journal of Economic Perspectives*, which challenged some of the wilder "New Economy" assumptions that were popular at the time. A gentle and courteous man, Zarnowitz concluded: "The arguments in favour of a new Golden Age are generally not very persuasive."[12] Zarnowitz argued that long business expansions benefited society by cutting unemployment and increasing prosperity but they also made the economy unbalanced and were therefore difficult to sustain. Sooner or later economic activity would reach a peak and start falling – in other words a recession would begin. When the article appeared the US economy was entering its eighth successive year of growth. In the final quarter of 1998 GDP had expanded at a stunning annual rate of 6.7 percent. Zarnowitz's warning did not go down well. "Everyone was tremendously optimistic. I rejoiced with everybody else because I know that recessions are really bad for business and for workers but I was skeptical," he says. "I was one of the few that didn't believe it would last and unfortunately I was right on that ... It's very unpopular to predict a peak, of course. Cassandras are unpopular and that is a reason, I believe, why peaks are not more promptly recognized."[13]

Zarnowitz has endured far worse than merely playing Cassandra in a robust academic debate. In the United States he is best known as a University of Chicago professor emeritus and an authority on the business cycle. Less well known is that he was born in southern Poland in 1919. A decade before World War Two his family settled in a town called Oświęcim, the German name of which is Auschwitz. Zarnowitz lost most of his family there, but he and his brother fled to eastern Poland, then under Soviet control.

He survived 19 months in a succession of Soviet labor camps, unlike his brother who died in one. In 1946 he arrived in a camp for "displaced persons" near the German university town of Heidelberg, where he studied economics while waiting for a US visa. Six years later he emigrated to the United States.

A primitive point of view

Perhaps Zarnowitz's experience helps him to take a more considered view while others get caught up in the excitement of the day. "We don't know how to eliminate recessions and a boom is no answer. A boom is temporary," he says. "All these booms were accompanied by these ultra-optimistic assessments that the business cycle is dead, we'll have permanent prosperity and non-inflationary too. It's a very primitive point of view."

> **Forecasters may feel it's better to miss a recession if everyone else does, than to go out on a limb, forecast one that fails to materialize and get public egg on your face.**

Apart from the Cassandra effect there's also a question of probability: recessions are relatively rare so forecasting growth is a pretty good bet in most years. In his study Loungani found that only 15 percent of the total country-years (the number of countries multiplied by the number of years in the study) were marked by a recession. A "herding" tendency may also play a role: forecasters may feel it's better to miss a recession if everyone else does, than to go out on a limb, forecast one that fails to materialize and get public egg on your face.

At the City Business School in London, Roy Batchelor notes that there are exceptions to the Cassandra theory: the professional pessimists. If they stick at it long enough one of Loungani's recession years will pop up eventually. "It's not true people are reluctant to forecast recessions," he says. "It's quite hard to get the consensus to come up with a recession but if you look at individual forecasters one or two make their reputations by forecasting recessions continuously. Every decade or so they're heroes." These Heroes of Recession feature in Chapter 10.

Another message from the Loungani study is that economists make much bigger errors forecasting "emerging markets" – poorer nations in Latin America, Eastern Europe, Africa and Asia – than they do with wealthy developed states. "In the past the forecasts have been way too optimistic for the emerging markets. At some point a dose of reality will be needed," he says. For example, every year forecasters predicted the Ukrainian economy would start growing the following year and every autumn reality would dawn. "They would stick to that positive forecast all the way through to October, realize it's going to be another negative year, mark down that year and say it's going to be positive the following year." Economic theory says that countries starting from "a low base" ought to grow 6 to 8 percent a year when events turn in their favor. But events have not turned in favor of many emerging economies like Ukraine. Forecasters seem reluctant to heap more bad news on nations benighted by economic dislocation and poverty. "For the emerging markets and the developing countries there seems to be a tendency to try and give them the benefit of the doubt, boost up their prospects to the extent that you can," says Loungani. "But you can't keep giving up on the credibility of your forecast just to give them a chance."

Loungani's work studies only average forecasts and how well, or badly the "consensus" performed. This leaves the old question of whether any individuals are better at foreseeing downturns. Do any star economists stand out from the crowd? A team of economists at the Swedish central bank, the Riksbank, tried to answer this question in a study of no fewer than 52,000 forecasts of GDP and inflation. The predictions, produced by 250 institutions from 1991 to 2000, cover six countries: the United States, Japan, France, Germany, Italy and Sweden. As we know, Alan Greenspan is unlikely to win any prizes for predicting but the Riksbank team proved what anecdote suggests: the most renowned forecasters do not necessarily make the best forecasts. In fact this is a headline in the study.[14]

The most renowned forecasters do not necessarily make the best forecasts.

A herd that survives but rarely excels?

"For most countries in this survey it is not the most renowned institutions that are the top performers in forecasting. Indeed it is often rather anonymous and less known banks and associations that top the rankings," the Riksbank economists said in the report. For example, in Japan the Wall Street giants JP Morgan and Merrill Lynch were among the best at predicting inflation and GDP, but the Tokai Bank, little known outside Japan, had better GDP forecasts while the mean average forecast – the much maligned consensus – was best overall trade-off between inflation and GDP. Indeed in Japan and Italy the average forecasts are better than most individual forecasts. Although this wasn't the case in the other countries it nevertheless suggests that it's wrong to deride the consensus as a herd which survives but rarely excels. "Using the consensus mean may be a sound strategy. It is a fairly safe bet: rarely the best but displaying a stable reliable performance," they said. And what about the outsiders, the forecasters who shun the safety of the herd? "Some forecasters that dare go against the mainstream can perform systematically better than the average view. In ranking the forecasters, however, it is important to remember that there is no guarantee that a track record of superior forecasts necessarily means that this state of affairs will continue." Back we come to the old problem. Some lone wolves will usually do better than the pack but we know who they are only after events have vindicated their forecasts and when it is too late to act on them. To mix metaphors, this year's champion may well languish mid-league next year. Zarnowitz backs this argument. "If you take an average over five years or so ... then you find that consensus forecasts beat individuals," he says. "Individuals are superior to the median but they will not be consistently superior. They are just by chance."

One crumb of comfort for the forecasters: the study found that at least they consistently outperformed the "random walk" or naïve forecast of merely entering this year's actual GDP change or inflation rate as next year's forecast. This may sound like damning with faint praise but don't forget that their colleagues who try to predict currency exchange rates (in fact it's often the same people) usually do worse than a flip of the coin. Unfortunately the study found one exception: Paris-based Banque Indosuez managed to predict French inflation worse than the random walk.

Perhaps the strongest message from the Riksbank is that we shouldn't necessarily believe all we hear on television or read in the newspaper. That includes some of the best known forecasters such as the IMF itself and the Organization for Economic Cooperation and

Development, a Paris-based club of the world's wealthiest nations. "Those that are often accorded considerable weight in the media,

We shouldn't necessarily believe all we hear on television or read in the newspaper.

such as the IMF and the OECD, rank amongst the less successful forecasters," it said. "This points to the need of regularly assessing the forecasting performance of institutions. Only in this way will forecasters' influence in the public domain stand in proportion to the quality of their assessments."

Bubble trouble

After the failures of the 1990–1991 recession US economists ought to have been on their guard a decade later. In early 2000 the economic expansion became the longest in American history; that inevitably focused minds on how much longer it could last. "Everybody knew sooner or later it had to come to an end so all the forecasters were far more alert than they have been in the past," says Loungani. Up to a point. Polls of Wall Street's biggest banks and brokerages conducted by Reuters show that economists may have talked a lot about a possible recession, but very few stuck their necks out by predicting one until it had already begun. The same old story.

In July 2000 reporters at Reuters New York bureau rang economists at all 29 banks and brokerages, domestic and foreign, that deal directly in US government bonds with the Treasury. The question was: what is the percentage likelihood of a recession in 2001? Stand up HSBC Securities, which deserves a prize for Wall Street's best recession watcher of the year. The London-based bank put the chances at 60 percent. In fact HSBC had

Percentage likelihood of US recession in 2001			
Primary dealer	**2001** (% chance)	**Primary dealer**	**2001** (% chance)
ABN AMRO Inc	less than 25	Goldman, Sachs	10
Banc of America Securities	20	HSBC Securities (USA)	60
Banc One Capital	10	J.P. Morgan Securities	25
Barclays Capital	30	Lehman Brothers	less than 25
Bear, Stearns & Co	0	Merrill Lynch Govt Securities	5
BMO Nesbitt Burns	20	Morgan Stanley Dean Witter	25
Chase Securities	25	Nomura Securities Int.	20
CIBC World Markets	10	Paribas Corp	less than 10
Daiwa Securities	0	Prudential Securities	20–25
Deutsche Bank Securities	10	SG Cowen Securities	n/a
Dresdner Kleinwort	20	Zions First National Bank	15
Fuji Securities	0		

Source: Reuters poll published July 7, 2000

Table 5.2 *Forecasts of likelihood of US recession in 2001*

warned its clients the previous June when it issued a 51-page report called "Bubble Trouble," listing 12 symptoms of a bubble economy. The United States fulfilled all 12, wrote HSBC's economics chief Stephen King. Perhaps the less said about the others the better. Of the 22 firms in the poll that made a prediction, none apart from HSBC put the chances of recession in 2001 at more than 30 percent. The average was just 17.5 percent (Table 5.2).

Reuters repeated the survey through 2000 and into 2001, but Wall Street was painfully slow to acknowledge the approaching downturn. A poll published on December 19, 2000 – less than a fortnight before recession year – showed that HSBC had raised its forecast to a 70 percent likelihood while Credit Suisse First Boston put the chances at 50–50. All the others still believed that on balance the United States could dodge a downturn in 2001

Percentage likelihood of US recession in 2001			
Primary dealer	**2001** (% chance)	**Primary dealer**	**2001** (% chance)
ABN AMRO Inc	20	Goldman, Sachs	33
Banc of America Securities	35	Greenwich Capital Markets	15
Banc One Capital	20	HSBC Securities (USA)	70
Barclays Capital	30	J.P. Morgan Securities	25
Bear, Stearns & Co	10	Lehman Brothers	10
BMO Nesbitt Burns	33	Merrill Lynch Govt Securities	10
CIBC World Markets	35	Morgan Stanley Dean Witter	None
Credit Suisse FB	50	Nomura Securities International	40
Daiwa Securities America	40	Paribas Corp	15
Deutsche Bank Securities	40	SG Cowen Securities	25
Dresdner Kleinwort Benson	20	Salomon Smith Barney	35
Fuji Securities	30	UBS Warburg	30
		Zions First National Bank	20

Source: Reuters poll published December 19, 2000

Table 5.3 *Forecasts of likelihood of US recession in 2001*

(Table 5.3). The average likelihood of recession was less than 28 percent.

A couple of days later a US investment strategist at Morgan Stanley, Peter Canelo, was optimistic about the coming year. "Sure the economy will slow down but there won't be a recession," he said. Wall Street is building a base for another bull market. Most of the action will come in the first half of 2001."[15]

Some time in the following three weeks, Morgan Stanley underwent a major change of heart. On January 8, 2001 its Chief Economist, Stephen Roach, broke ranks with the other big US firms and predicted that the US economy would contract 1.25 percent in the first half of the year. Roach executed this volte face in style, defending his views the following month at a testy debate with two of his peers, John Lipsky of JP Morgan Chase and Bruce Steinberg at Merrill

Lynch. "We have an economy that's gone so far out on a limb with respect to excesses, it's not even funny," Roach said. "Recessions serve the purposes of purging excesses and that is what this recession is all about." Steinberg scoffed at the notion. "The so-called excesses of our economy are actually quite limited," he said. "The doom and gloom scenario is overdone." In response Roach cast himself as the Cassandra. "We work for securities firms that sell these things called stocks. A recession is not a popular call."[16]

It was a call that Jack Guynn, President of the Federal Reserve Bank of Atlanta, was not prepared to make. In January 2001 he boasted that the US economy was the "envy of the world" and predicted it would grow about 3 percent that year, albeit with a slight rise in unemployment. "In the long term, though, I think the moderation of growth that we'll witness in 2001 will be a mostly healthy thing," said Guynn.[17]

But at Fed headquarters in Washington Alan Greenspan clearly didn't want to take any chances this time: the Fed cut interest rates twice in January 2001. Greenspan wasn't about to predict a recession; such a suggestion might be self-fulfilling from so powerful a man. But, as ever mangling the English language along the way, he accepted the possibility. "Whether it, in and of itself, is enough to actually induce a significant contraction which, in retrospect, we will call a recession is yet too early to make a judgment on," he told a congressional committee.[18]

It took the horror of September 11 to wake Wall Street up to the downturn that had begun six months earlier.

It took the horror of September 11 to wake Wall Street up to the downturn that had begun six months earlier. Hard though it may be to believe now, in a Reuters poll conducted in late June only three firms – HSBC, Morgan Stanley and Bear Stearns – put the chances of a recession in 2001 at over 50 percent. Finally in a poll published on September 21 every firm accepted what now seems the blindingly obvious – that America was in recession. As late as the start of October Treasury Secretary Paul O'Neill, anxious perhaps to keep up national morale, still maintained a recession could be avoided.[19]

However, a few days later even O'Neill seemed to accept the inevitable. All that remained was the solemn confirmation of the end to America's longest economic expansion. On October 31 the Commerce Department reported annual GDP had fallen in the three months ended in September. On November 26, 2001 Zarnowitz and his colleagues on the NBER's Business Cycle Dating Committee formally declared that the economy had peaked in March that year, and therefore this country was in recession.

Notes

1 Interview with author.

2 The NBER has a table of every peak and trough of the US economy since the mid-19th century on its website at www.nber.org/cycles/recessions

3 The Russian economy grew a marginal 0.9 percent in 1997 but went back into recession in 1998. Source for these figures is the International Monetary Fund's World Economic Outlook.

4 Interview with author.

5 Memo on the recession issued by the Business Cycle Dating Committee of the National Bureau of Economic Research on January 10, 2002.

6 "Further cross-country evidence on the accuracy of the Private Sector's Output forecasts," by Grace Juhn and Prakash Loungani, IMF Staff Papers, forthcoming.

7 Interview with author.

8 This research was published in a report to clients of Charterhouse Securities Ltd, UK: Economics, Revisions to Growth, February 2001.

9 Letter to *Financial Times*, published December 21, 2000.

10 "There will be growth in the spring: how credible are forecasts of recovery?" by Prakash Loungani, *World Economics*, Jan–March 2002.

11 Interview with author.

12 "Theory and history behind business cycles: are the 1990s the onset of a golden age," by Victor Zarnowitz. NBER Working Papers No 7010, March 1999, published in the spring 1999 edition of the *Journal of Economic Perspectives*.

13 Interview with author.

14 "How good is the forecasting performance of major institutions?" by Mårten Blix, Joachim Wadefjord, Ulrika Wienecke and Martin Ådahl. Penning- och valutapolitik, 3/2001, available at www.riksbank.se/upload/5874/blix_mfl_2001_3.pdf

15 Quoted by Reuters, December 22, 2000.

16 Debate at Council on Foreign Relations and interview with Reuters, both February 8, 2001.

17 Speech to Atlanta Rotary Club, January 8, 2001.

18 Testifying to House of Representatives' Financial Services Committee, February 28, 2001.

19 Previewing congressional testimony by O'Neill Treasury spokeswoman Michele Davis told a news briefing on October 1, 2001: "The third quarter may be negative but the fourth quarter doesn't have to be if we take the appropriate policy steps." He was right: fourth quarter GDP grew 1.7 percent.

6

Verdict on the IMF

"The prominent role as forecasters often accorded to the IMF and the OECD in the media may be unwarranted."

– From a study by economists at the Swedish central bank

In May 1997 the International Monetary Fund forecast the Indonesian economy would grow a healthy 7.5 percent the following year, enough to ensure that the nation's poor could look forward with some hope to 1998. In fact the economy contracted no less than 13 percent: 1998 turned out to be a depression year of appalling hardship for ordinary Indonesians and it wasn't that much better for President Suharto. He was forced out of power after 32 years of autocratic rule.

The Asian crisis, which began in Thailand in 1997 and spread like a plague through the region in the following year or so, caught most forecasters on the hop. In the 1990s the emerging economies of East Asia enjoyed spectacular growth rates and in early 1997 few people saw any strong reason why that should not continue. Nobody foresaw the phenomenon of "contagion," when investors took fright and abruptly pulled out of countries not only across Asia but also in Eastern Europe and Latin America. Money flooded out of nations as diverse as South Korea, Russia and Brazil which had little in common beyond the fact that they were all classified as emerging economies. Yet it was the IMF's lack of foresight that particularly drew criticism. Is the IMF, which twice yearly publishes forecasts for around 90 countries in its World Economic Outlook (WEO), worse than anyone else?

Research shows that it is but opinions vary on how much. "It is evident that the accuracy of the private sector's forecasts is in almost every case a little bit better than that of the WEO forecasts," said Prakash Loungani in his research paper.[1] "The differences are marginal in the case of forecasts for industrialised countries (particularly current-year forecasts) but rather more substantial in the case of developing countries." The Riksbank, which looked only at forecasts for six wealthy nations, is less charitable towards the IMF and the OECD. "In all six countries they both fared considerably worse than the mean (average prediction)," the Swedish economists wrote. "Our results thus indicate that the prominent role as forecasters often accorded to the IMF and the OECD in the media may be unwarranted."[2]

IMF forecasts are not merely there to grab media attention. They are also an important part of the economic advice that the IMF dishes out to member states.

That policy advice that the IMF offers governments is not always popular; it often demands austerity which inflicts great suffering on the poor. For instance, the IMF led a $47 billion rescue package for Indonesia, but its tough line on scrapping subsidies provoked food riots. Plenty of people are gunning for the IMF and bad forecasts risk undermining the credibility of the rescue packages themselves.

The policy advice that the IMF offers governments is not always popular; it often demands austerity which inflicts great suffering on the poor.

Guy Meredith, an IMF economist, disputes whether the forecasts and the policies are bad. "There is a risk that people may think our record is significantly worse than a typical record, and I don't think that's the case. The danger is the perception that we're lousy forecasters also means we're lousy economists and lousy policy advisers," he says. "There are cases where our forecast errors may have contributed to ex-post if not ex-ante policies that weren't optimal but I don't think that's generally the case. And I don't think that if one had used private sector forecasts in those cases that one would have come to much different conclusions on the policy."[3]

None the less the IMF recruits top class economists so why should they lose their touch as forecasters, at least compared with their private sector colleagues, once they arrive at its headquarters a few minutes from the White House? The IMF belongs to its member states; is it a case of he who pays the piper calls the tune? Do governments lean on IMF economists to massage the forecasts? "Firmly this is an independent forecast, this is the product of the IMF," says Tam Bayoumi, an IMF division chief who is responsible for the World

Economic Outlook.[4] "Our basic job is to interact with governments. They are the people we provide our assessments to, they are the people we give our policy advice to. In a situation like that there are clearly close contacts, but the Fund has a strong internal review process which is designed to avoid forecasts being unduly influenced by the interaction between country teams and the authorities."

Bayoumi accepts that IMF forecasts for Africa have been consistently overoptimistic, partly due to the disasters, man made and natural, which hit the continent too often. "Nobody is going to predict that their country will have a war or a drought but we know that in all of Africa, sadly, the chances of it happening to a country or two is significant," he says. But such bias isn't exclusive to public sector organizations. "The private sector is basically trying to flog shares ... I would not be fully convinced that there are no biases in private sector forecasts."

Nevertheless it can't be easy playing Cassandra in an institution as powerful as the IMF. For instance, the IMF's Chief Economist, Kenneth Rogoff, made himself few friends in Washington when he proclaimed that a recession in the United States was a "done deal."

It can't be easy playing Cassandra in an institution as powerful as the IMF.

Rogoff, a nervous academic from Harvard University, made the comment at his first news conference in the job on September 26, 2001 – just as US officials from the President down were trying to piece together Americans' morale after the attacks a fortnight earlier. Rogoff withdrew the prediction before the news conference had even ended although, of course, it turned out to be correct.

Conspiracies could explain overoptimistic forecasts, but the IMF can also err on the pessimistic side. After the disastrous experience with Indonesia in 1998, the IMF predicted the economy would shrink another 3.4 percent the following year. In the event it grew, albeit by a marginal 0.8 percent. Another explanation of the IMF's poorer forecasting record is the lumbering nature of the beast. When private bank economists revise their forecasts they can let their clients know with a quick round-robin e-mail or an update to their weekly bulletin. International organizations move less nimbly. The *World Economic Outlook* normally appears only twice a year to coincide with meetings of finance ministers from member nations in May and October. The internet has allowed publication to be brought forward a few weeks but even then the WEO is hardly hot off the press. The forecasts go to the IMF's executive board for approval as early as the beginning of April and the beginning of September before heading to the printers. "You've got what's called an October forecast that's really been close to finalised in mid August. You can make changes but you have to have a powerful reason for making changes," says Meredith. "We're a couple of months behind the curve."

Never did that time lag catch out the IMF more than in the autumn of 2001. When Rogoff held his news conference he presented forecasts which had been well overtaken by events. "We explicitly decided not to try to incorporate the effects of the attacks on New York," says Meredith. "There were no data available and again it's not acceptable for us to take a shot in the dark and ... mark world growth down by a percentage point." In the event the IMF did just that.[5] It could hardly stand by such outdated predictions for the best part of half a year until the next regular update. So it issued some revised forecasts in

November 2001 and published an "interim" WEO in December foreseeing a very different world. It cut global economic growth in 2002
from 3.5 percent to 2.4 and its prediction for the United States tumbled to 0.7 percent from 2.2. For Japan the revision turned growth of
0.3 percent into a contraction of 1.0 percent.

But Meredith feels that it is the emerging economies which pose
the biggest problems for all forecasters at the IMF and elsewhere.
"We understand even less the dynamics in emerging markets. The
political and economic shocks are greater for these countries so
the variance of GDP growth is higher. The predictability of contagion
is pretty low. We're working on early warning systems, as everybody
else is, for financial crises," he says. "It's hard to find a general
model that's very good at predicting financial crises but we continue to look."

Notes

1 "Further cross-country evidence on the accuracy of the Private
   Sector's Output forecasts," by Grace Juhn and Prakash Loungani, IMF
   Staff Papers, forthcoming.

2 "How good is the forecasting performance of major institutions?" by
   Mårten Blix, Joachim Wadefjord, Ulrika Wienecke and Martin Ådahl.
   Penning- och valutapolitik, 3/2001, available at
   www.riksbank.se/upload/5874/blix_mfl_2001_3.pdf

3 Interview with author.

4 Interview with author.

5 Meredith was interviewed before the IMF published its revised
   forecasts.

7

Rate watch

"People have described (monetary policy making) as like driving a car in fog and trying to steer by looking in the rear view mirror. That's a pretty good description."
– Charlie Bean, Chief Economist, Bank of England

National economies are made up of millions, tens or even hundreds of millions of people. How those individuals and businesses spend or save their wealth, if they have any, largely determines how quickly economies grow or contract. On financial markets buying and selling by thousands of people – or millions on the biggest stock exchanges – determines whether prices rise or fall. Anyone trying to predict economies and markets must try to factor in the behavior of large numbers of people who may not always act rationally. But official interest rates should be a different kettle of fish. In many nations a dozen or so central bankers, largely middle-aged or elderly men, set interest rates at regular, scheduled meetings. Of course the policymakers at institutions such as the US Federal Reserve and the European Central Bank are hostage to events like anyone else. They react to changes in the economy and on markets, or better still try to pre-empt them. But most want to set interest rates as predictably as possible, or at least say they do. It wasn't always so but these days transparency is the watchword in monetary policy. Leading central banks have medium-term strategies for setting interest rates and often drop hints, ranging from the cryptic to the broad, about their intentions. Surely this is a near paradise on earth for forecasters: to predict interest rates all they need to do is read the minds of a handful of people, many of whom are happy to lend a helping hand? Alas the lot of the central bank watcher is not so simple.

These days changes in interest rates make big news. Central bank governors like Alan Greenspan, who a generation ago remained obscure civil servants, have become headline makers. They are powerful people who exercise great influence over the economies they guide. When they raise rates credit card holders cringe and savers rejoice; when they cut them the tables are turned. Governments often have to fight tooth and nail to get their tax and spending plans through parliament or congress. By contrast many central bankers change their policies without deferring to anybody; until a few years ago the Federal Reserve didn't even tell anyone until weeks after   the event. Therefore it's unsurprising that Market Prophets predict their every move.

National authorities have two ways of influencing their economies: fiscal policy and monetary policy.

National authorities have two ways of influencing their economies: through fiscal policy and monetary policy. "Loose" fiscal and monetary policies usually encourage economies to grow faster, possibly at the risk of rising inflation; "tight" policies tend to subdue growth and inflation but can, if excessive, tip economies into recession. Fiscal policy determines levels of taxation and public spending and is usually announced in annual government budgets. Monetary policy aims to control the supply of money in the economy by setting interest rates. In the past many governments set both policies but over the years they have ceded control of interest rates to their national central banks. In the United States, the Federal Reserve system was created in 1913 although its independence was not formalized till the 1950s; Germany, haunted by hyperinflation in the 1920s when politicians controlled the money supply, created an independent central bank after World War Two, the Bundesbank. However, the Bank of England became operationally independent only in 1997, and the Bank of Japan a year later. In 1999 the European Union went a step further. Most of its member nations handed over interest rate powers to a supranational body, the European Central Bank, which sets a single, "one size fits all" monetary policy for all the countries which adopted the euro currency. Three of the fifteen EU members, Britain, Sweden and Denmark, have refused to join in so far.

Decisions by central bankers affect the lives of millions of people. They don't control economies, no individual or group does, but they influence them. If they think an economy is growing too fast they raise interest rates to prevent inflation. That raises the cost of borrowing so consumers and companies alike scale back their spending financed by loans, and save because of more attractive interest rates. If the central bank does its job well, economic growth will fall gently to a sustainable rate and inflation will subside. The opposite also holds true. If a central bank senses inflation is not a threat but growth is at risk it will cut interest rates. Cheaper borrowing encourages consumers and companies to spend

Decisions by central bankers affect the lives of millions of people.

and invest more, thereby stimulating the economy. Of course central banks sometimes fail: recessions happen from time to time and economies sometimes overheat.

Investors and traders on financial markets follow the central banks closely because interest rates affect the value of shares, bonds and currencies profoundly. Most leading central banks have committees which set rates according to a published schedule, ranging from fortnightly at the Bank of Japan to eight times a year at the Federal Reserve (although the Fed in particular sometimes drops cuts out of the blue between scheduled meetings). Much ballyhoo accompanies announcements of the outcome because financial markets try to price in rate changes just as they anticipate economic data.

Reading the runes

On January 3, 2001 the Fed provided a textbook example of how markets behave when caught on the hop. At about 1 pm, just as many in the markets were grabbing a sandwich from the delis of Manhattan, the Fed cut its benchmark target for the fed funds rate from 6.5 percent to 6.0. Markets were caught unawares: no regular meeting of the Federal Open Market Committee (FOMC), the Fed body that sets monetary policy, was scheduled until the end of the month. It hadn't cut rates for more than two years and hadn't changed them at all for eight months. Indeed the cut was the biggest for over eight years. A tide of euphoria swept the stock market. By the time it closed that afternoon the Standard & Poor's index of 500 leading stocks had jumped 5 percent while the Nasdaq composite, a measure of volatile high-technology shares, had rocketed no less than 14 percent. We now know the rally was not to last but any trader who was caught on the wrong side of this blip lost a lot of money.

Currencies and bonds are also sensitive to shifts in monetary policy while on derivatives markets traders bet directly on future interest rates. Therefore a specialized branch of financial forecasting has developed over the decades: central bank watching. Every big financial institution has a resident analyst, sometimes a team of them, whose job is to read the runes, to predict how the men at the big central banks (plus the occasional woman, but it's a conservative business) will set rates in the weeks, months and years to come.

The work of central bankers is often arcane and Greenspan is everyone's idea of a senior civil servant. Dark-suited and well into his seventies, he uses such an impenetrable dialect of central bank-speak that frequently few people understand what he's trying to say; apparently that includes his wife, television reporter Andrea Mitchell. He reputedly had to propose marriage three or four times before she finally understood what he was getting at. Yet he is rated the second most powerful man in the United States after the President and credited with delivering a decade of inflation-free prosperity from 1991 to 2001.

A fog of secrecy

Until recently central bankers around the world worked in a fog of secrecy, and believed that they did their job better as a result.

Until recently central bankers around the world worked in a fog of secrecy, and believed that they did their job better as a result. But they have realized in the past decade – sometimes on their own, sometimes after persistent prodding by politicians – the need to allow the outside world a limited glimpse of their work. Before 1994 the Fed took weeks to announce that it had changed its target for the fed funds rate. Until then Fed watchers were not so much occupied with forecasting what it would do in the future as with trying to work out what it was doing in the present. They had to scrutinize the Fed's actions in its daily operations on the money market for signs of whether it was forcing the fed funds rate up or down. On February 4, 1994 the Fed surprised everyone by announcing its decision immediately after a regular meeting and a year later it wrote this step towards greater openness into its rules. The Bank of Canada began announcing scheduled interest rate meetings as recently as 2000. Before then its rate changes would fall from the blue.

This creep towards transparency undoubtedly helps central bank watchers to forecast rate moves better, although their skills would be redundant if monetary policy became too predictable. "I don't want my life made too easy; otherwise I won't have a job," says Danny Gabay at JP Morgan Chase in London.[1]

There's little chance of central banks ever becoming too predictable. Central bankers sift reams of data for clues on how the economy may develop and like private sector economists they find that the statistics too often say more about the past than the future. At the Bank of England Charlie Bean applies a motoring metaphor to setting interest rates. "People have described it as like driving a car in fog and trying to steer by looking in the rear view mirror. That's a pretty good description," he says.[2] So central bankers have to apply large amounts of judgment to interpreting the data. Sometimes it's gut feeling based on experience but they also rely on their forecasts. Here transparency has its limits. Some central banks such as the Bank of England publish regular, detailed forecasts of GDP and inflation; others such as the Fed are less forthcoming. This means that economists must try to burrow into the minds of the people who make the decisions. There's no use in an analyst interpreting data as demanding a rate rise if the policy-makers think the same figures justify a cut. To understand the psyche of a central bank analysts need to know as much about its aims, strategy and tactics as possible. Only if it's fairly open about the way it works is this possible.

> **Central bankers don't yield up secrets out of the goodness of their hearts, to make life easy for analysts so everyone can make more money on the markets.**

Central bankers don't yield up secrets out of the goodness of their hearts, to make life easy for analysts so everyone can make more money on the markets. Two other forces are at work: those of democracy and those of self-interest and credibility. Greater openness is a trade off for the limited democratic accountability to which unelected central bankers are subject. Also, contrary to a belief which was once almost universal, the more predictable monetary policy is, the better it is likely to work.

In a democracy voters can eject politicians from office if they make a mess of economic policy, and sometimes do. But they have no direct power to show the door to incompetent central bankers. Alan Greenspan acknowledges the case for democratic accountability. "Openness is an obligation of a central bank in a free and democratic society. US elected leaders chose to vest the responsibility for setting monetary policy in an independent entity, the Federal Reserve. Transparency of our activities is the means by which we make ourselves accountable to our fellow citizens to aid them in judging whether we are worthy of that task," he said.[3]

The glare of the press

A more practical argument for openness is that it helps, rather than hinders, central bankers in their work. Greenspan, one of the more conservative of his peers, seems to think the Fed has set policy successfully despite its near glacial creep towards greater openness, rather than because of it. "In recent years, we have achieved a far better balance, in my judgment, between transparency and effective monetary policy implementation than we thought appropriate in the past," he said. Note that transparency counterbalances rather than complements effective monetary policy. In Greenspan's book transparency should stop well short of opening the Fed's workings to the media's gaze. "The undeniable, though regrettable, fact is that the most effective policymaking is done outside the immediate glare of the press."

Despite their image of power central banks directly control only short-term interest rates which they manipulate or set in regular market operations. All other rates, including those that often have the greatest effect on stimulating or subduing the economy, are set by the markets. For instance the Bank of England decides monetary policy through its repurchase or "repo" rate, which it charges on two-week loans to commercial banks in daily money market operations. In Britain rates of interest on home mortgage loans tend to move up and down with the repo. When the Bank of England tightens monetary policy mortgage interest payments rise for many homeowners, meaning they have less money to spend in the economy. When the Bank cuts rates, many Britons have more cash to spend. But in the United States mortgages rise and fall with long-term rates, not the fed funds rate that Greenspan and his colleagues control. Something similar applies to businesses. If they need money to build a new factory they'll borrow it for 10 years, not for two weeks or 24 hours.

If central banks are to influence the economy effectively they must ensure that changes in short-term rates are transmitted quickly into the cost of long-term borrowing. They must influence the expectations of financial markets and here, according to Fed Vice Chairman Roger Ferguson, lies the case for transparency and predictability. "If the monetary authority can be clearer about what it is doing now and what it plans to do – not in the sense of setting future moves in stone, but rather in terms of explaining risks that might influence future policy – then market participants can improve their expectations of future short [term] rates," he said. "Transparency ought to bring the rates that matter most for the macro economy into closer alignment with the intentions of monetary policymakers. In effect, greater transparency allows policymakers to work with the market, not against it."[4]

Hell hath no fury like a wrong-footed financial commentator

If a central bank works well with markets its credibility tends to rise. If traders and investors believe it can run monetary policy effectively that belief by and large becomes self-fulfilling: interest rates across the spectrum will rise and fall in tandem with changes in official short-term rates. Better still markets should anticipate central banks' moves, so that the process of boosting or subduing the economy has already begun when the news breaks; the sooner the better because monetary policy takes time to work in the real economy. Bruce Kasman, a Fed watcher at JP Morgan Chase in New York, estimates that US GDP takes between 6 and 18 months to react to rate changes. The lag for inflation is even longer at 18–36 months. Economists liken this to taking a shower. If you turn up the hot tap it takes a while for the hot water to come through and similarly there's a delay when you try to cool the flow. Central bankers must judge what effect their decisions will have on the economy anything from six months to three years ahead. As in the shower, if they get things wrong the economy may get scalded or a cold shock.

As in the shower, if they get things wrong the economy may get scalded or a cold shock.

Over the years there have been economic shocks aplenty. In the 1970s and 1980s it was sudden jumps in oil prices, in 2000 it was a bursting of the stock market bubble and the following year it was the attacks on America. The last thing central banks should do is spring nasty surprises of their own. The Bank of England is particularly keen to avoid this. "One source of shocks to the economy can be erratic monetary policy. As a central bank what we want to achieve is as stable an economic environment as we can," says Bean. "It doesn't mean there's never going to be any shocks," he says. "But at least we're taking erratic monetary policy out of the equation." Mervyn King, the Bank's deputy governor, puts it differently. "We do not want to surprise people. Policy should be boring and predictable," he said.[5]

How boring and predictable are the world's leading central banks? If predictability equates to transparency the record seems patchy. In May 2001 Reuters published a survey in which 62 central bank watchers gave them marks out of 10 for transparency. The Bank of

England came out top with an average 8/10, closely followed by the Fed and Bank of Canada. The Bank of Japan was well adrift with five and the European Central Bank limped in last with 3.8. At the time the ECB was going through a particularly rough patch in its relations with financial markets, having sprung a couple of surprises on them. That spring it left interest rates unchanged when most ECB watchers had predicted a cut, and then promptly lowered them when no one was expecting a move. Was the poll a fair judgment or a knee jerk reaction from a bunch of economists who had got egg on their face?

Was the poll a fair judgment or a knee jerk reaction from a bunch of economists who had got egg on their face?

the poll a fair judgment or a knee jerk reaction from a bunch of economists who had got egg on their face? "There's an element of self-interest here," says Gabay. "The markets are there to make money and when they're unhappy it means they're not making money. That's because they feel they're not being given a level playing field by the ECB." The Bank of England's Governor, Eddie George, once paraphrased Shakespeare to put it another way. "Hell hath no fury like a wrong-footed financial commentator," he joked.[6] As we'll see later the ECB subsequently managed to wrong-foot not only economists but also the Bank of England itself. One wonders whether George found that so amusing.

Fed watching: one man counts

Not so long ago the Fed was secretive in a manner more appropriate to a police state than a democracy. "The need for and appropriateness of such secrecy was virtually unquestioned," said Ferguson. "It was part of the culture of central banking. Indeed, the one word of advice for a new central banker was probably 'mystique'." This mystique helped the central bankers to cultivate an image of near omnipotence and infallibility which, naturally, was false. The Fed created a language of its own designed not to communicate but to confuse. In a recent report on central banks a group of senior economists and bankers defined "Fedspeak" as "the use of numerous and complicated words to convey little if any meaning."[7] Greenspan raised Fedspeak to an art form twice a year when he testified to Congress. The report recalls an occasion when a senator claimed to have understood what the Fed chairman had just said. "In that case," replied Greenspan, "I must have misspoken."

> **The Fed created a language of its own designed not to communicate but to confuse.**

One of the report's authors is Alan Blinder, one of five Fed vice chairmen and women to have served in Greenspan's mighty shadow. Blinder says the pressure to bring policymaking more into the open gradually built up but he was usually in a minority of one or two when he argued for it in the mid-1990s. "It was not popular then and I took my bumps and bruises arguing for greater transparency," he says.[8] Blinder, who returned to his job as a professor of economics at Princeton University in 1996, chaired a committee on the issue. "It was very hard to get agreement within the committee and when it came to the full FOMC the suggestions for greater openness were basically rejected."

Good people making good judgments

But in recent years Greenspan has mellowed. He manages to get his message over, although still more by nudges and winks than the Bank of England and European Central Bank, which have formal rules for communicating with financial markets. "If you were coming down from Mars and looked at the three institutions, it may look like the Fed is the least transparent. The Fed does things based not on rules but on institutional experience," says Kasman. "Monetary policy is really an art, not a science. If you watch the way Greenspan has acted it's a tremendous confirmation that what you need is not good rules, but good central bankers. It's a judgment game and you need to have good people making good judgments."

Greenspan sends signals to the market in his speeches, statements and congressional testimonies. They're still coded but these days they can usually be deciphered. Blinder, who also served on President Bill Clinton's Council of Economic Advisers, says this rapport is due partly to Greenspan's longevity – he has been Fed chairman since 1987. "The markets have gotten used to his style," he says. "He does make these hints which, if you're a neophyte, seem totally cryptic but if you're a professional Fed watcher they become modestly clear, [although] I wouldn't say they become crystal clear ... He used to pride himself on being totally obscure. He doesn't do that any more and I think he genuinely tries, in his own way, to give very strong hints about which way the Fed is heading."

The Federal Reserve System has seven governors who sit on the board in Washington, plus 12 regional reserve banks in major US cities. Interest rate policy is set by the Federal Open Market Committee, on which the governors and the president of the New

York Fed have permanent seats. Heads of the other regional Feds fill the remaining four seats, serving one-year terms on a rotating basis. Officially the FOMC meets in Washington eight times a year to set interest rates, so every six weeks or so markets around the world hold their breath as they await the outcome. The US economy dominates the world economy and the Fed is a dominant force in setting its course, so interest in the Fed's moves runs far beyond the borders of the United States. At times of urgency or crisis Greenspan has called telephone conferences of the FOMC between the regular meetings and dropped rate cuts on to unsuspecting markets.

On the plus side the Fed publishes minutes of the FOMC meetings and records of how each member voted, but only after the following meeting, more than six weeks after the event. Since 2000 the FOMC has announced the "balance of risks." This reveals whether it's more concerned about inflation, economic weakness or neither. If inflation is more on the FOMC's mind the implication is that the next move in rates may be upwards; if economic weakness is the worry the next change may be a cut.

All this helps Fed watchers to predict rate moves but a major unknown is the Fed's precise objective. Its legal mandate is to achieve "stable prices" and "maximum employment." In practice the Fed tries to let the economy achieve the highest growth rate possible without excessive inflation. But what are stable prices? Other central banks have clear rules: for the ECB it means no more than 2 percent inflation. The Bank of England's mandate is even clearer: it targets 2.5 percent inflation and if the rate strays below 1.5 percent or above 3.5 percent the governor has to write a "mea culpa" letter to the government explaining why. But nobody knows what the Fed means by stable prices. In 2001 US inflation rose sharply and yet the Fed cut rates because it was worried about the looming recession. "They have been perfectly willing to run with 3.5 percent headline inflation while simultaneously presenting this as a state without inflation," says Klaus Baader, an economist at Lehman Brothers. "In Europe with 3.5 percent inflation the ECB would have found itself under enormous pressure."[9]

Maestro Greenspan

The Fed values this power of discretion that many of its peers lack. Wayne Angell, who was a Fed governor from 1986 to 1994, doubts that the Fed will accept a precise inflation target. "Not while Greenspan's there. He prefers it to be the way it is," says Angell, who now works at the Wall Street firm Bear Stearns. "It's a lot harder to do monetary policy the way he tries to do it when the Fed is responsible for the growth rate, the rate of unemployment and price stability. He's more actively judged to be a maestro if he does something very hard than if he does something very simple."[10]

Greenspan chairs the FOMC in a way that can make life tough for other members.

Greenspan chairs the FOMC in a way that can make life tough for other members. For instance Blinder, appointed vice chairman by Clinton in 1994, quit more than a little frustrated after only two years. Later he diplomatically described the Fed as "extremely chairman-dominated."[11] But Greenspan's status as much more than a first among equals makes life simpler for anyone who has to forecast the Fed. Analysts sometimes find themselves bombarded by conflicting opinions from different policy-makers at the ECB particularly, but that's not a problem with the Fed. "Greenspan is certainly the key player and if you're able to figure out what he's doing that's enough," says David Greenlaw, a

Fed watcher at the Wall Street giant Morgan Stanley.[12] But that doesn't guarantee success. "In a lot of cases, however, you're not able to figure out what he's doing. Probably his main trademark is flexibility and that makes it hard to figure out whether there's a core position that he's always going to fall back on. I don't think there is."

Nevertheless, in contrast to some ECB watchers, Fed watchers feel that their central bank is ultimately on their side. "The Fed has a strong desire not to wrong-foot the market. That doesn't mean the Fed is going to tell the market what it is going to do but it's going to leave the range of surprises within a boundary," says Kasman. "It believes fundamentally that it does its best work when the market is understanding what its actions are and why it's taking actions. As a result of that you get more bang for your buck in terms of transmitting policy."

Once in a while Greenspan does surprise Fed watchers by cutting rates between scheduled meetings. Usually the rationale is that the need is urgent. In central banking a stitch in time saves nine. But Greenlaw, himself a former Fed economist, suspects that sometimes the surprise may be deliberate. In the late summer and early autumn of 1998 anxiety beset financial markets after Russia defaulted on part of its debt, setting off a chain of events that brought Long-Term Capital Management, a huge hedge fund, to its knees. On September 29 the Fed cut rates to steady nerves but it wasn't enough. The next FOMC meeting wasn't scheduled until mid-November. A fortnight later the Fed struck again, lowering the fed funds target between scheduled meetings for the first time in four years. "I think they were going for some shock value in that easing. They were trying to stabilise markets and they were really trying to surprise people by going inter-meeting. It wound up being successful," says Greenlaw.

For all his empathy with the markets, Greenspan falls well short of total predictability. "We shouldn't exaggerate, he doesn't completely telegraph," says Blinder. "Having the markets surprised by the central bank's decision is not a financial calamity, although some traders will lose money on it. Central banks ought to be trying to minimise those surprises rather than maximise them as a general rule." Nevertheless the Fed made no less than three unscheduled cuts in 2001 as the recession set in.

State secrets

One way of discovering how a central bank sees the future, and is therefore likely to act on interest rates, is to study its economic forecasts. Here the Fed is less than forthcoming. Its staff update their forecasts before all eight FOMC meetings a year but they are published only twice a year. Blinder has little patience for this but believes the cause is not yet lost. "Frankly I think it's a disgrace that they treat their forecasts as if they were state secrets. There's no reason to do that," he says. "I wouldn't rule out that changing in the Greenspan period. That's the kind of small, incremental change towards transparency that he's shown himself willing to make."

The United States has a political system that vests great power in the hands of one man, the President. In central banking terms it's therefore unsurprising that Greenspan, rather than the FOMC, has accumulated so much power. He has probably earned it. After presiding over a decade of uninterrupted growth, many Americans put great faith in his ability to guide the economy through the storm that followed. But vesting so much power in the man rather than the system brings its own uncertainties. Greenspan's predecessor, Paul Volcker, was also a commanding personality, but you don't have to go too far back to find a weak Fed chairman. Many Fed watchers regard William Miller, appointed by President Jimmy Carter in the 1970s, as a failure. So what happens when the leader departs? "There's a quite substantial risk [when] Alan Greenspan gets replaced by someone else, and that day will eventually come. The old system that was totally personalised to Greenspan will not be transferable," says Blinder. "You may see a period of time when it's similar to what the ECB has been going through almost since its inception, where the markets often feel they've been wrong-footed because they've misunderstood the messages coming out of Frankfurt. We could have some of that here in the US if the Greenspan replacement, whoever he is, is not particularly deft." Life for the Fed watcher may not be so easy after the maestro leaves the rostrum.

ECB watching: one council counts

While the Fed is the world's most influential central bank, the European Central Bank must be its most controversial.

Many ECB watchers believe their life is already far from easy. While the Fed is the world's most influential central bank, the European Central Bank must be its most controversial. Rightly or wrongly Greenspan is the most admired central bank chief, while the ECB's President, Wim Duisenberg, is the most criticized. Analysts argue the rights and wrongs of ECB interest rate decisions but they do that with many central banks. Where they single out the ECB for a special roasting is the old chestnut of predictability. Whereas the Fed appears to be largely predictable, the ECB seems anything but. "The ECB's relationship with the markets is troubled and strained. The primary reason is lack of transparency," says Gabay. "There's a general sense that the market doesn't really understand what the ECB is doing or thinking. The ECB itself seems to change its mind and seems to be struggling to find an identity."

The ECB is a child of European monetary union and is therefore the junior member of the central banking family, in age rather than size. It has officially controlled monetary policy only since the euro was born at the start of 1999 but it sets interest rates for almost 300 million people in 12 countries, more than the population of the United States. Monetary policy decisions are made by an 18-member council which comprises six officials based at the ECB's headquarters in Frankfurt plus the heads of the 12 national central banks. The council usually meets once a fortnight but since the autumn of 2001 it has made interest rate announcements only once a month. The ECB's primary mandate is to ensure price stability, and unlike the Fed it has defined what that means: keeping inflation on the harmonized index of consumer prices below 2 percent in the medium term. In other words the ECB can allow inflation to stray above 2 percent but not for too long. To achieve this it has created more of the rules that the Fed eschews, in the form of a two-pillar strategy. The first pillar is growth of M3 money supply, for which it has set a "reference rate" – ECB officials avoid calling it a target or a ceiling – of 4.5 percent a year. If growth of the supply of money is kept under control this will keep consumer prices in check further down the road, or so monetarists believe. The second pillar is a wide range of other indicators such as growth, the employment rate, financial market developments and economic forecasts made by ECB staff.

The ECB's achievements are already considerable. Nagging doubts had long surrounded the euro project, which was a huge step into the political and economic unknown, and a political row over who should lead the ECB only made things worse. A year before monetary union there were almost as many different interest rates as there were countries preparing to adopt the euro. In Germany the key interest rate was 3.3 percent, in Italy it was 5.5 percent and in Ireland over 6 percent. But on December 3, 1998 the ECB moved decisively to sort out the mess, staging a coup that stunned financial markets. Under ECB leadership all but Italy set their rates at a common 3 percent. Financial markets had never seen anything like it; but there never had been anything quite like European economic and monetary union. Duisenberg, a gruff Dutchman with a shock of white hair, allowed himself a little self-congratulation. "Central banks are always accused of acting too late and too little. This time we shall not be accused of acting too late. I am very happy that we came to this decision. It is a unique decision. I expect it to be received rather sensationally," he said.[13]

On January 4, 1999 the euro began trading and soared to $1.18 on the currency markets. Away from the public gaze a new euro zone-wide money market began operating smoothly. The ECB and Duisenberg could scarcely have enjoyed greater credibility. But it didn't last long. Almost immediately the euro began sliding against the dollar. This probably had less to do with the ECB's stewardship than the US boom which sucked money out of Europe. But as the euro dropped ever further Duisenberg began to feel the heat. In April 1999 the ECB, having fought off heavy political pressure to cut rates for months, did just that, lowering its refinancing rate by a sizeable half percentage point to 2.5 percent. Memories fade fast and many people recall this as a total surprise. In fact ECB watchers had predicted it in a Reuters poll shortly beforehand but only by a slim majority, and few had expected such a large drop. It was the first of the surprises that have provoked hostility among traders and ECB watchers, the people who have lost money and face respectively as a result.

Not much straight talking

Greenspan is regarded as successful largely because of his rapport with, not his antagonism towards, the markets. But the ECB has trouble in getting its message over. "It's the manner in which they're communicating that has people upset. That's been reflected through a weaker currency. The markets have chosen to beat up the euro as a sign of disapproval. There is a sense that whenever the ECB starts talking the euro starts falling," says Gabay.

Fallen it certainly has. The euro lost approaching a third of its launch value before hitting rock bottom at 83 US cents in October 2000. Unpredictability, it seems, carries a price. Ironically, the last great slide in the euro was probably due to too much rather than too little openness. In September 2000 the ECB persuaded the United States and other governments of the Group of Seven (G7) nations to mount a joint intervention to buoy the euro. This was the intervention that caught out Tony Norfield and most other currency forecasters. Although the blitz succeeded Duisenberg blotted his copybook the following month by frankly discussing G7 currency strategy in a newspaper interview. The case for transparency in interest rate policy enjoys wide support but there is an unwritten rule that central bankers should never discuss currency intervention in public, at least not in advance. G7 nations have large currency reserves but they are nevertheless dwarfed by the global market. In the September intervention the G7 nations spent an estimated $6 billion in buying euros, but that compared with average daily turnover on the currency markets of about $1.3 trillion. The only way for intervention to work was to hit speculators out of the blue so that they suffered losses and would think twice about pushing the euro even lower. An element of surprise is crucial but Duisenberg seemed to have forgotten that.

This episode underlines a paradox of central banking. Greenspan rarely talks on the record to the media, and limits his appearances to relatively few speeches and testimonies to Congress. Yet he gets his message over. By contrast senior ECB officials talk to the media frequently and still seem to struggle sometimes to communicate. Duisenberg usually holds a news conference once a month after ECB council meetings, and gives regular speeches and interviews, as well as testifying to the European Parliament. Scarcely a day seems to go by when one or another council member does not pop up. But quantity doesn't always mean quality. "They do a fair amount of talking but not a great deal of straight talking," says Baader.

"ECBspeak" resembles the language of real people more than Fedspeak, but it still needs careful interpretation. Here's an example of a comment Duisenberg made in October 2001 when inflation was running well above the reference rate: "We expect inflation to fall below two percent early next year. Now, if future developments would change that assessment in a way that it would fall earlier or further in particular than currently assumed, then there would be room for manoeuvre in monetary policy." Translated into English this means that markets shouldn't expect an interest rate cut soon because inflation won't fall below target for a while, but we might change our mind if things turn out better than expected. Or does it? When people talk so vaguely they're inevitably misunderstood sometimes. Greenspan gets away with it because Fed watchers have got used to his Delphic utterances over the years. But the ECB has no such track record even though most of its governors are experienced central bankers.

A cacophony of opinions

Events in the spring of 2001 offer a fine example of how more communication doesn't always mean better communication. At the time most other leading central banks had cut interest rates due to signs that the global economic growth was slowing down, and pressure was growing on the ECB to follow suit. Duisenberg, the ECB's Chief Economist Otmar Issing and the chiefs of the two most powerful national central banks, Bank of France Governor Jean-Claude Trichet and Bundesbank President Ernst Welteke, all weighed in with hints. Some seemed to signal a rate cut was imminent, others that it was not, but ECB watchers ended up believing that it would move in April. Nothing happened and everyone began to give up hope of a cut. So certain did ECB watchers become that in a Reuters poll they gave a 96 percent likelihood of no rate change when the council met on May 10. The ECB obliged by cutting the refinancing rate from 4.75 to 4.50 percent. Amid uproar Duisenberg flatly denied that council members had contradicted each other, describing the ECB ensemble as a

> **More communication doesn't always mean better communication.**

"harmonious chorus." ECB watchers felt otherwise. "It was a cacophony of opinions," said Ditmer de Vries, an economist at Rabobank in the Dutch city of Utrecht.[14]

Deciphering Greenspan's comments is an essential part of Fed watching, but some ECB watchers have almost given up on Duisenberg and colleagues. "If you listen too much to what ECB council members say they will lead you in the wrong direction," says Michael Schubert, an economist at Commerzbank in Frankfurt. "Analysts can't decide what weight to give to their reasoning. It's an extremely uncomfortable situation for us."[15] For the medium term Schubert relies solely on his own forecasts of economic growth, inflation and so on, and then decides whether they warrant a cut, a rise or no change in interest rates. But until late 2001 the ECB made rate decisions every fortnight and economic models cannot be this precise. To predict the outcome of specific meetings Schubert had no choice but to rely on comments from ECB officials. Their guidance, however, proved less reliable than his own judgment. "That's the reason why my performance in predicting rate decisions in the very short term is very bad. In the longer term it's much better," he says.

A silly game?

This begs the question of whether the ECB deliberately throws analysts off the scent. "I hope I'm incorrect in the slight suspicion that there may have been some preference for surprising the market," says Charles Goodhart, a former member of the Bank of England's Monetary Policy Committee. "I think it's a silly game. You get more efficiency with a central bank if markets appreciate what you're trying to do."[16] Issing, the ECB's chief economist, rejects the idea. "It is sometimes suggested that central bankers occasionally set out to 'trick' the markets into expecting one policy outcome and then deliver a quite different one," he said. "Let us be quite clear that a monetary authority which did this would merely increase volatility in the financial markets and damage its own credibility. It would do nothing to aid the smooth conduct of monetary policy and the pursuit of price stability."[17]

Most economists give the ECB the benefit of the doubt. "There have been occasions when the signals from the ECB have been completely in the other direction from the subsequent policy move," says Ken Wattret, an ECB watcher at BNP-Paribas bank in London. "I tend to think it's accidental. I do think it's a presentational issue."[18] Despite the tensions many economists are sympathetic to the ECB's difficulties. "You can list a whole host of reasons why the ECB faces more problems than the others," says Wattret. For a start most central banks find setting the right policy for one country hard enough; the ECB has to do it for 12. Another problem lies in the European preference for consensus. It's unlikely that the ECB system would tolerate such a dominant figure as Greenspan. European Union institutions are built on the concept that every country, large or small, gets a say. The result is that the ECB council is relatively large. It can't be easy to get 18 members from 12 countries to agree a common line and say the same thing in public, all in their own languages. And so it goes on. One result of the ECB's multi-national nature is that it is secretive about what goes on at its interest rate meetings. The Fed, Bank of Japan and Bank of England all publish minutes of theirs and records of how committee members voted. But the ECB fears that in this case transparency would spell trouble.

"If detailed minutes and voting records were published, the discussions of the collegial Governing Council would certainly become less frank and open-minded," said Sirkka Hämäläinen, an ECB council member from Finland. "There would be a risk that the necessary euro area-wide thinking of the individual members of the Governing Council would be discouraged if they were subject to pressure from the domestic public."[19] Put less politely the fear is that rival blocs of countries might form and split the ECB council, a potential disaster for a project which requires everyone to subordinate their national interest to the good of the euro zone as a whole.

In a step forward for predictability the ECB began publishing economic forecasts in 2000, but only twice a year and in the form of wide ranges. In the first batch the ECB forecast that the euro zone economy would grow 2.6–3.6 percent in 2001. Most economists simply took the mid-point of the range, 3.1 percent, to be the ECB's view on growth and inflation. Incidentally, even this wide range didn't stop the forecast from being way too optimistic. GDP actually grew a paltry 1.5 percent.

Issing has said that the occasional surprise cannot be avoided but has produced evidence from bond rates to show that markets believe the ECB will keep inflation below 2 percent in the long term. "ECB policy has always been credible and has usually been predictable. By and large the communication strategy with the markets has worked surprisingly well for a new institution," he said.

Notwithstanding the statistics and the ECB's uniquely difficult position, the men and women from Frankfurt still have an ability to annoy. One Frankfurt economist – who asks to remain anonymous for fear of appearing to have deserted his post – recalls another surprise the ECB sprang on September 17, 2001, a few days after the attacks on America. That morning Duisenberg said it was too early to judge whether the horrors of the previous week would affect European economic growth. Economists took that to mean the ECB would not follow a rate cut the Fed made that day. But the ECB seems to have changed its mind: that afternoon it lowered its benchmark rate to 3.75 percent. The reason, it said, was that the attacks on America had worsened the outlook for economic growth. It was another example of the ECB doing the right thing the wrong way. "I was so furious I just shut down my computer. I felt my work here is in vain and I went home," said the Frankfurt economist.

The Bank of England: nine individuals count

The Bank of England has yet to reach the blissful state of boring predictability that it strives to, but it's not for the want of trying by policymakers at its magnificent, if sombre, Georgian headquarters on Threadneedle Street. "We don't like surprising the markets, we don't deliberately want to do it," says Bean. "That's one of the reasons why we don't like having inter-meeting moves." But on September 18, 2001 – one week after the attacks on America – the Bank's Monetary Policy Committee did just that.

> **The Bank of England has yet to reach the blissful state of boring predictability that it strives to, but it's not for the want of trying by policymakers.**

Surely at this terrible time it was entitled to spring a surprise for the common good? Paradoxically the MPC cut the repo rate for the first time between official meetings to *avoid* springing a surprise, but it did so reluctantly.

The US stock market had closed after the World Trade Center attack and the Fed acted to calm panicky investors by cutting rates shortly before it reopened on September 17. Although made between regular meetings most Fed watchers had predicted the move. What came next was less well anticipated. Late in the day the ECB made the unexpected cut that so frustrated the Frankfurt economist, and raised expectations that all the leading central banks would follow suit by announcing that it had acted "in concert" with the Fed. Switzerland and Sweden, two sizeable economies outside the euro zone, heightened these expectations by following the ECB's lead. But what about the Bank of England, nicknamed the "Old Lady of Threadneedle Street?"

Bean explodes the myth, if ever there was one, that the central banks acted in a carefully coordinated operation. September 17 had got off to a predictable start but then events took an unexpected turn. "The Fed action was not surprising. Although it was between meetings it was entirely expected. If we had been in their shoes we would probably have had an inter-meeting change because it was made quite deliberately to underpin the US markets when they reopened," says Bean. "However … it was more surprising to see the ECB acting and making what is a relatively big change for them." Switzerland and Sweden had followed suit not because they were taking part in a coordinated operation but because they wanted to keep their currencies as stable as possible against the euro.

Where was the Old Lady?

So, come the morning of Tuesday September 18 the Old Lady felt rather alone. The MPC had almost no data yet on whether the attacks had hurt British economic confidence, so members wanted to wait till the next scheduled meeting when the picture might be clearer. But that wasn't for another fortnight and expectations were building rapidly. "We were in this position where lots of central banks were moving and there was discussion in the press the next day 'Where was the Old Lady?'. There was certainly an expectation that we were going to move even though we weren't scheduled to meet," says Bean. "We had been surprised by the ECB's move late on the Monday and we were then in the position that if we didn't move on Tuesday it would be a surprise to the markets. We didn't have a lot of alternatives."

Normally unscheduled rate changes surprise markets; this time not making one would have surprised them. The MPC therefore met on the Tuesday morning and, trying to achieve a semblance of normality, it announced the cut at noon London time, when decisions of regular meetings are revealed. "Central banks often tell other central banks shortly before they actually move," says Bean. "But it's relatively rare to have a deliberately coordinated decision where everybody changes rates together. If you're going to have that, the logical thing is for them to announce it at the same time. In this case there was no attempt to have a deliberately coordinated action." Like economists at commercial banks, he was clearly unimpressed with the message from Frankfurt. "As far as the ECB is concerned, most of their monetary policy decisions have actually been defensible from where I stand. Where I think there has been an issue is in communicating the rationale for their decisions." Restrained this may be; one can only imagine what the vocabulary was like at the Bank when the ECB announced its surprise.

In reality the Bank of England can spring surprises like anyone else. In August 2001 no one expected it to change rates, at least none of the 26 economists in a Reuters poll predicting the outcome. Yet it did just that, cutting the repo rate from 5.25 to 5 percent. What no one in the markets knew was that the MPC had cut its forecast for global economic growth, which meant that inflation would be less of a threat in Britain. Only the following week was this revealed in the quarterly inflation report. "No one pretended that the decision was easy," said Deputy Governor King. "In itself, it was unfortunate that we sprang a surprise but the Committee was faced with a choice – to surprise people last week by cutting rates, or to surprise them today by publishing a forecast which indicated that a further cut was likely."[20]

Another pitfall for Bank of England watchers is that they may well forecast a rate decision before the MPC members have made up their mind. Sometimes, says Bean, the case is clear cut enough that he goes into meetings having decided how to vote. But more often than not central bankers have to weigh up conflicting evidence and conflicting demands of the economy. In recent years Britain has suffered a "two-speed" economy. Manufacturing industry has struggled while retailers and companies providing services have enjoyed a boom that risks pushing up inflation. What should the MPC do? Cut rates to help the manufacturers or raise them because of the services boom? The answer is rarely black and white; the task of the central banker is to interpret shades of grey and make a tough decision. Bean admits to sleepless nights during difficult meetings, which he tackles with sleeping pills from the United States. The MPC has its hawks and doves but also an undogmatic "soft centre" of members who like to hear the arguments before deciding how to vote. "It's not the case

The answer is rarely black and white; the task of the central banker is to interpret shades of grey and make a tough decision.

that you go in having already made up your mind," says Bean, one of the MPC's swing voters. "If we had all made up our minds before we went into the room there wouldn't be any point in having the meeting."

Taking what individual MPC members say in isolation can be as misleading as anything emerging from ECB headquarters. In September 1999 one of the MPC's doves, Sushil Wadhwani, issued a plea to "give growth a chance" – only for the committee to put rates up a few days later. However, there is a fundamental difference between central banking, London and Frankfurt style. The ECB believes in collective responsibility, meaning that every council member is supposed to follow the party line. By contrast the MPC is a committee of nine individuals who speak only for themselves. Therefore woe betide any MPC watcher who takes the views of Wadhwani or King, a renowned hawk, to reflect the majority view.

Nevertheless it's conventional wisdom among central bank watchers that it's harder to predict the ECB than the Bank of England. Economist Michael Dicks at Lehman Brothers has produced evidence using market interest rates going back to 1992 to prove not only this, but also that the ECB is less predictable than the Bundesbank, which set interest rates for Germany before monetary union.[21]

Bang goes a myth

So much for the markets but evidence from the pundits suggests the case is far from clear cut. Before each Fed, ECB and MPC meeting Reuters asks analysts to forecast the outcome. As with most statistics much depends on how they are presented but analysis of the poll results from 1999 to 2001 shows that the ECB may be more predictable than many people assume. In absolute terms central bank watchers did make more wrong forecasts for the ECB than the others. But this ignores an important consideration: the ECB held about twice as many meetings as the MPC and three times as many as the Fed. The Bank of England meets monthly and the Fed every six weeks or so, but until late 2001 the ECB decided rates fortnightly. So it is only fair to express the pundits' success rate in percentage terms. Here the ECB looks more predictable than the MPC and gets much closer to the Fed.

In the years 1999 to 2001 the pundits made seven wrong calls for the ECB, six for the Bank of England and one for the Federal Reserve. That means they either failed to forecast a rate change or forecast one when none materialized. If you tighten the definition of a correct call to include also the size of the move the picture is even clearer: the ECB watchers were wrong 11 times, MPC watchers eight times and Fed watchers two times. But in percentage accuracy terms the numbers are turned on their head, at least with the ECB and MPC. The Fed watchers still had the best record on moves but the ECB watchers came in second and their MPC colleagues last. Using the tighter definition the "league" positions remained the same (Table 7.1). Bang goes a myth which Goodhart never believed anyway. "It is not clear ... that the Bank of England beats the ECB on predictability. If anything it tends to be the other way," he says.

These results exclude changes at unscheduled meetings because no polls were conducted immediately beforehand. Between 1999 and 2001 the Fed made three unscheduled cuts, two of which were unexpected and one (on September 17, 2001) which was anticipated on markets. Incorporating these assumptions makes the success rate of Fed watchers on direction alone a more ordinary 88.5 percent, little different from the much maligned ECB.

	Federal Reserve	European Central Bank	Bank of England
Direction only			
No. of correct forecasts	22	64	30
No. of incorrect forecasts	1	7	6
Total number of forecasts	23	71	36
Percentage accuracy	**95.7**	**90.1**	**83.3**
Direction and size of change			
No of accurate calls	21	60	28
No of wrong calls	2	11	8
Total number of meetings	23	71	36
Percentage accuracy	**91**	**85**	**78**

Source: Reuters Polls 1999–2001

Table 7.1 *Interest rate forecasting: the record. The upper table shows how often economists correctly forecast changes in official rates. The lower shows how often they also correctly forecast the size of the changes*

Bank of Japan:
different rules count

Bank of Japan watching is a game where different rules count. Most major central banks have a clear strategy of controlling inflation and promoting economic growth by changing interest rates. But in Japan there is no inflation to control – prices have fallen since the late 1990s – and, it can be argued, no interest rate policy to change, at least until deflation has been conquered. Some Bank of Japan watchers even feel they are scarcely BOJ watchers any more: they must scrutinize the government more because it alone has the power to pull the country out of the deflationary mire. Such is the topsy-turvy world of Bank of Japan watching.

In structure and recent history the BOJ looks similar to some of its peers. Until 1998 the BOJ, like the Bank of England of old, officially agreed monetary policy with the government, although the Ministry of Finance had by far the bigger say. However in April 1998 a new law guaranteed the BOJ effective independence in "the pursuit of price stability, contributing to the sound development of the national economy." The BOJ set up a nine-member policy board, appointed by the cabinet, which comprises officials from the central bank plus economic and financial experts from outside.

Here the similarities start running out. In the 1990s the Japanese economy, which had seemed unbeatable in the 1980s, ran into serious problems. Speculative bubbles on the stock and property markets burst, burdening the banking system with a mountain of bad loans – debt on which borrowers could not afford to pay interest or repay the capital. Banks suffered another blow as steady falls in Japanese share prices eroded their capital bases. Japanese banks became "risk averse"– they were reluctant to make new loans for fear that they would never see their money again. Credit is the lifeblood of any economy but in the late 1990s bank lending began falling and by the end of 2001 it had dropped for four straight years. With the economy beset by problems neither ordinary Japanese nor companies were keen to take on new debt anyway. Japanese consumers, who account for 60 percent of the economy, slashed their spending and put the money in the bank. Starved of consumer spending and loans to fund expansion the economy ground to a

Japanese consumers, who account for 60 percent of the economy, slashed their spending and put the money in the bank.

near halt. At best the 1990s were years of weak economic growth, at worst of shrinkage. In 2001 the economy slipped into its third recession in a decade and, in a country where workers were once used to jobs for life, unemployment rose to record levels above 5 percent of the workforce.

At first the Bank of Japan did what any other central bank would have done: it cut interest rates. In fact it kept cutting them until it could go no further. At the start of 1991 the official discount rate was 6 percent and by 1995 the BOJ had lowered it to 1 percent. That year it began targeting the interest rate charged on overnight lending, the equivalent of the US fed funds rate, so a BOJ watcher's job was to watch how the central bank managed this rate. Throughout the decade the government also did its bit, pumping huge amounts of money into the economy especially through public works projects, but with little success.

At the end of the decade things went from bad to worse: deflation struck. High inflation, as many nations discovered in the 1970s and 1980s, can damage economies badly and that is why most central banks have a mandate to keep it under control. But deflation can also wreck businesses and entire economies. When prices fall a company's revenue falls too but many of its costs don't necessarily follow suit immediately: it still has to pay the rent, energy bills and, of course, salaries. Deflation tends to destroy profits so that many companies go out of business. Others slash their costs to survive, usually by laying off workers en masse. Unemployment shoots up, the jobless have less money to spend on goods and services and this pushes prices yet lower. Deflation can spiral downwards just as inflation can spiral upwards. The Great Depression provides a sombre example. Between 1929 and 1933

US prices fell 50 percent, accompanied by mass unemployment and immense social deprivation. Deflation is also a great disincentive to spending. Anyone who put dollars under their mattress in 1929 would have found their money worth twice as much in 1933.

The ZIRP

Nothing like the Great Depression has happened in Japan and many countries would be happy with 5 percent unemployment. But deflation causes trouble even in its milder forms. In early 1999 the BOJ therefore flooded the market with money to prevent deflation taking a grip and Japan entered the Alice in Wonderland world of super-low interest rates. In March the overnight rate slumped to 0.03 percent and in October the BOJ officially said that it had adopted a "zero interest rate policy," nicknamed the ZIRP, to remain until deflation had been overcome. Eighteen months later the BOJ thought it had detected a glimmer of light in the economy and raised rates for the first time in a decade, targeting a 0.25 percent overnight rate. Politicians were horrified, fearing that the modest rise would snuff out any recovery. They were right and in March 2001 the BOJ chose another new target, setting a minimum level of money in accounts which commercial banks hold at the central bank. The idea was to shower the banks with money again in the hope they would lend it out for investment and consumption that would finally get the economy moving. But much of the money simply sat in the bank accounts unused. In late 2001 the BOJ's target was more than six trillion yen but at some points the banks were keeping double that in their accounts. This tended to make the target largely academic, but the BOJ vowed to continue targeting reserves until prices had at least stabilized, or started rising. In December 2001 the BOJ raised the target to 10–15 trillion yen.

So how do BOJ watchers go about their job in this ever curiouser world? Interest rates, the bread and butter of any other central bank watcher, are practically irrelevant under the present regime. "What the BOJ is doing now is quite different from what other central banks have done in history," says Hiromichi Shirakawa, chief economist at UBS Warburg in Tokyo. "BOJ watchers are not looking at interest rate policy. There is no interest rate policy at the Bank of Japan."[22] From time to time the BOJ changed the reserve target in the way that other central banks change interest rates but this had only a tiny effect on interest rates and even less on the overall economy.

There are two schools of thoughts on Japan's predicament. One is that the BOJ should print even more money to kill deflation; the other is that no amount of money supply can cure the fundamental problems of the Japanese economy and particularly the banking system.

There are two schools of thoughts on Japan's predicament. There is no shortage of ideas offered to the BOJ for boosting the money supply, such as that it should buy foreign bonds, some of the banks' bad loans or even stocks or property – anything to create inflation and get the economy moving. But by 2001 the BOJ's Governor Masaru Hayami felt that the BOJ had run out of ammunition. "I cannot readily say what further steps are available," he said.[23]

All this knocked the ball back into the court of the politicians and bureaucrats at the Ministry of Finance to sort out the mess. Analysts predicting Japanese monetary policy could no longer rely on pure central bank watching. "We are basically not BOJ watchers," says Shirakawa, who for many years was an economist at the BOJ. "We are closely monitoring how the government and the Ministry of Finance view the currency, view interest rates and view inflation, because eventually they are going to decide the course of monetary policy as well."

Nevertheless, no one can ignore the BOJ altogether, so how predictable is it? Naka Matsuzawa, chief investment strategist at Nomura Securities in Tokyo, says not very much but this reflects the unusual times. "The BOJ is not using conventional measures, it's not just raising interest rates or lowering interest rates," he says. "Inevitably it becomes unpredictable."[24] In many ways the BOJ is a transparent institution. Governor Hayami regularly testifies before parliamentary committees, press conferences are held after the fortnightly board meetings and minutes are published about a month later. The BOJ has also started publishing economic forecasts. But Matsuzawa says that in another sense the BOJ is less transparent because politicians, mainly powerful figures in the ruling Liberal Democratic Party, and bureaucrats from the Ministry of Finance can influence BOJ decision making, even though it is officially independent. This sometimes leads to ECB-style changes of mind. "Of course the economy is evolving and we have had a huge problem with the financial and banking system," says Shirakawa. "I wouldn't say that changing views are always due 100 percent to political pressure [but] ... my sense is that 50–60 percent is. In that sense it's not so independent."

Despite the unusual times, the BOJ does try to prepare markets for big changes. For instance, officials flagged the interest rate rise of 2000 weeks in advance, saying openly they wanted to scrap the ZIRP and leaving only the timing uncertain. Indeed in the week before the move Hayami conducted a public slanging match with the government over the wisdom of raising rates. This was one occasion when the BOJ's independence was unquestioned.

One day deflation will be defeated, inflation will return and BOJ watching will revert to something akin to central bank watching in the rest of the world. "But not within the coming few years," says Shirakawa. "It will take two, three, maybe four years." The clock is ticking.

Notes

1 Interview with author.

2 Interview with author.

3 Speech via videoconference to the Federal Reserve Bank of St. Louis, Economic Policy Conference, October 11, 2001.

4 Speech to the National Economists Club and Society of Government Economists, Washington, D.C. April 19, 2001.

5 Interview with *The Sunday Times*, May 16, 1999.

6 Speech at the Mansion House, London on June 11, 1998. A week earlier the Bank of England had made an interest rate rise that almost no economists had predicted.

7 *How Do Central Banks Talk?* By Alan Blinder, Charles Goodhart, Philipp Hildebrand, David Lipton and Charles Wyplosz, published jointly by the International Center for Monetary and Banking Studies, Geneva, and the Centre for Economic Policy Research, London, 2001.

8 Interview with author.

9 Interview with author.

10 Interview with author.

11 Quoted by Reuters, June 3, 1999.

12 Interview with author.

13 Interview with *Financial Times*, December 4, 1998.

14 Quoted by Reuters, April 6, 2001.

15 Interview with author.

16 Interview with author.

17 Speech to ECB Watchers' Conference, Frankfurt, June 18, 2001.

18 Interview with author.

19 Speech to conference in Helsinki, September 14, 2001.

20 Opening remarks at Bank of England news conference, August 8, 2001.

21 Testing ECB Credibility, Global Economic Monitor, August 17, 2001.

22 Interview with author.

23 Addressing press conference, November 21, 2001.

24 Interview with author.

8

Fame

"Fame is like a river, that beareth up things light and swollen, and drowns things weighty and solid."

– Francis Bacon, Essays

At the height of Wall Street's technology mania a certain Thomas Bock predicted the thousand dollar stock. Within a couple of years, he said, shares in a British internet company called QXL.com would rocket 15 fold to $1000. Even in the frenzied atmosphere of April 2000, this startling recommendation made everyone sit up, listen and, of course, buy. QXL.com shares briefly quintupled in value the day after Bock spoke before slipping back to end the session up a mere 100 percent or so. But who is, or was, Thomas Bock? Before this forecast Bock was a rookie analyst at a not particularly influential brokerage called SG Cowen. Few people knew him from Adam. But the thousand dollar stock made a great headline, meaningless though it was, and 28-year-old Thomas Bock became an instant Wall Street celebrity in the financial media. The lesson of this story of greed and gullibility is that Market Prophets don't just aim to make their clients rich by predicting well; they also aim to make

For many the surest route to wealth is fame.

themselves and their employers rich. Those who make the deals on Wall Street often prefer obscurity but those who sell forecasts have to stand out from the crowd. For many the surest route to wealth is fame.

Every generation on Wall Street produces its gurus, such as the colorful Joe Granville, but the technology boom of the late 1990s spawned a particularly large brood. The audience was bigger – more than half of American households had joined in by buying shares or unit trusts – and so too was the stage. No longer was market forecasting confined to the columns of the specialist financial press. Financial television channels such as CNBC offered live stock tips from celebrity analysts 24 hours a day. Recommendations and rumors spread like wildfire through financial websites and internet chat rooms. Never had it been technologically easier for analysts to reach a broad audience – provided they could make themselves heard above the din. For some the temptation to seek short cuts seemed too great to resist.

Bock was playing games. He issued his recommendation a day before QXL.com split its shares into three, a common practice to make stocks seem more attractive to small investors by reducing their price. So within 24 hours the $1000 forecast for QXL.com, an online auctioneer, had become a less headline-grabbing $333 forecast. Bock based his prediction mostly on the fact that eBay Inc, a US online auctioneer, had a stock market valuation of $25 billion at the time. Many people swallowed this hook, line and sinker. But even amid this irrational exuberance some brave souls suggested that Bock would do anything to get attention.

BOX 8.1

Need a forecast? Call the shrink!

When we need a market forecast, who do we turn to? A stock analyst, an economist? After what happened on the US stock market we might be better off calling a shrink. Psychology drives financial markets much more than we realize. Look at the Nasdaq, the electronic exchange which was home to the hottest stocks of the great technology bubble. At its peak in 2000 companies trading on the Nasdaq were collectively worth $6.75 trillion, that's almost 70 percent of the annual output of the US economy. But their revenues amounted to only 15 per cent of GDP and their net income a feeble 9 percent of corporate America's profits.[1] Yet, until the bubble burst in March 2000 people willingly bought these stocks, often in companies that never produced anything but heavy losses, at grossly inflated prices. Why?

The history of markets is littered with examples of irrational behavior from Dutch tulip mania in the seventeenth century onwards. The twentieth century produced three notable bubbles which inflated and, as sure as night follows day, burst: on Wall Street in 1929 and 2000, and in Japan in 1989. It works both ways: investors can also become irrationally depressed, and not only on the stock market. While America boomed the euro currency bombed. It lost almost a third of its value and nobody wanted to touch it. Were currency traders behaving any more rationally than the stock investors?

Much economic and financial theory assumes that humans act rationally and consider all information that's available before deciding to invest or divest. Perhaps this explains why the record of market forecasting is so poor. Some Market Prophets seek enlightenment in a relatively new field of science called behavioral finance.

This draws on psychology and other social sciences as it seeks to explain why investors behave as they do. Behavioral finance suggests:

- Investors give too much weight to recent experience when it contradicts long-term trends. When the Nasdaq rocketed they thought it would keep doing so indefinitely. In the long run shares rise only a few percent on average a year but they forgot about that.

- Investors become more optimistic when the market rises and more pessimistic when it falls. "Thus markets invariably move to overvalued and undervalued extremes because human nature falls victim to greed and fear," said Kirit Shah, former research chief at Sanwa International, a Japanese bank. In bull markets investors ignore the bad news and in bear markets they ignore the good news.

- Investors follow the crowd because it seems safer. As John Maynard Keynes said: "Worldly wisdom teaches that it is better for reputation to fail conventionally than to succeed unconventionally."[2]

- People overestimate their abilities; investors and analysts are particularly overconfident in areas where they have some knowledge.

- Investors often fail to bail out of a losing position because they're reluctant to acknowledge they've lost money. Although the US stock market fell by a third after March 2000 it wasn't until almost a year later that more money flowed out of mutual funds than into them.

So that explains why the high-tech bubble happened. Now, try building all this into next year's stock market forecast.

---

1 Behavioural finance and risks to risk management, by Kirit Shah, *The Euromoney Derivatives and Risk Management Handbook*, 2001/2.

2 *The General Theory of Employment, Interest and Money*, by John Maynard Keynes, 1936.

Nevertheless SG Cowen, which belongs to the French bank Société Générale, defended the work of its rookie analyst. "It was not a publicity stunt. It was equity analysis," said company spokesman Adam Brecht.[1] But he would say that. SG Cowen must have enjoyed its moment at the centre of a stage normally occupied by the likes of Merrill Lynch, Morgan Stanley or Goldman Sachs.

Bock was typical of a generation of young technology analysts, some of whom knew more about technology than about equity analysis, having worked only in the boom years of the 1990s. Wall Street's more experienced operators had little time for their youthful exuberance. "They've never been through a downturn," growled Frank Baxter, a veteran broker who had analyzed technology stocks in the 1970s and 1980s. "We'll sort out the analysts as well as the companies when there's a correction."[2] He was right. Within four months QXL.com shares had crashed to about $5 (the company is now called QXL Ricardo plc) and a year later Bock left SG Cowen, never to be heard of again.

Other analysts were more honest about the lure of fame. Joe Battipaglia became a frequent guest on financial TV as chief investment strategist at a small New York brokerage called Gruntal & Co. "We're all trying very hard to be recognized, to develop a following," said Battipaglia, who as a media pundit found himself hounded not for autographs but for stock tips in restaurants and airport lounges. "The very nature of our business is designed to get visibility, and the greater the awareness, the more successful we believe [our firms] become."[3] Especially for smaller firms without big marketing budgets, celebrity analysts bring free advertising and even a chance to get the company logo on TV. Employers, large and small, are willing to pay for that kind of success. According to the Securities Industries Association the average senior level research analyst made $280,637 in salary and bonus in 1999. That's not bad by real world standards but it's loose change in the world of Wall Street celebrity. According to the *Financial Times*, Mary Meeker, Morgan Stanley's "Queen of the Internet," made $15 million the same year.

Geeks with spreadsheets

Bock's moment in the limelight was brief. But others, notably a technology analyst called Henry Blodget, managed to last longer using similar tactics: Blodget's road to stardom was equally unlikely but typical of how Wall Street dropped its guard in the late 1990s. After graduating from Yale University with a degree in history, Blodget spent a year teaching English in Japan. Then he took up journalism only to abandon that quickly and head for Wall Street. Blodget had none of the conventional qualifications for a career on Wall Street: he never went to business school, he wasn't a chartered financial analyst and had little to offer in the way of experience. But in late 1998, as an analyst at the Canadian-owned investment bank CIBC Oppenheimer, he struck lucky. Blodget predicted that shares in Amazon.com, an online book seller, would hit $400. When he made the forecast the shares were trading at $240 but within weeks they had surged beyond $400 – sometimes gaining $60 a day – making Blodget a folk hero with the legions of small American investors. Merrill Lynch spotted the Blodget potential and hired him in early 1999 to replace an analyst who was inconveniently bearish called Jonathan Cohen. For a couple of years "King Henry," as he became known, surfed the high-tech wave, recommending a number of internet start-ups some of which, such as Pets.com and eToys, failed without ever making a profit. Amazon.com shares, by the way, closed 2001 at $10.82.

To be fair, King Henry did predict that 75 percent of dot.com ventures would fail, but it was the bullish forecasts that the investors remembered. It was good while it lasted but Blodget and Meeker, chief cheerleaders of the internet revolution, swiftly turned from heroes to villains when the bubble burst. In 2001 Merrill paid out $400,000 to settle an arbitration claim for $10.8 million. This alleged that overly bullish research from Blodget had lost a New York paediatrician half a million dollars earmarked for his daughter's college education. A few months later Blodget, a workaholic happier surfing the net than out partying with other Wall Street celebrities, announced he was giving it all up, aged 35, to write a book on the dot.com phenomenon for the publisher Random House. This was strange because Blodget had also announced two years earlier, in October 1999, that he was writing a book about the internet for Random House. With hindsight, Blodget made perhaps his most perceptive prediction near the height of the boom. "If the market should ever turn [down] people will go back to recognizing that we're all geeks with spreadsheets," he said. "And that's not particularly interesting."[4]

> If the market should ever turn people will go back to recognizing that we're all geeks with spreadsheets.

Blodget wasn't the only one to provoke lawsuits as the market turned sour. One law firm in Pennsylvania filed three suits naming Meeker and Morgan Stanley. These alleged that she had breached the "Chinese wall," a cordon sanitaire which supposedly divides the research and investment banking departments at financial institutions. When unbreached, Chinese walls allow analysts to issue gloomy forecasts on any company even if their investment banking colleagues are trying to land a big deal with the same firm.

Investors should be able to rely on analysts' research as objective and unbiased by the commercial interests of their employers. One of the lawsuits concerned the media giant AOL Time Warner. It alleged that Meeker had failed to disclose that her main job was to attract and retain investment banking clients for Morgan Stanley, which had "improperly earned millions of dollars in fees due to Meeker's behind the scenes deal making and business-generating activities." The suit claimed that "Meeker personally benefited from her improper conduct, which allowed her to purportedly earn $15 million in 1999 alone." US District Judge Milton Pollack threw out the lawsuits, calling them a collection of market gossip. Pollack also pointed out that analysts didn't get a share of investors' profits when the market rose, so why should they compensate investors for losses when the market fell?

No wealth without excess

Meeker defended her reputation with a report saying that despite a year-long sell-off, technology companies listed on the stock market since 1980 had created more than $2 trillion in wealth. "It's easy to shout about speculative excess but you don't get this kind of innovation and this amount of wealth created without the excess," she said. "People knew this was risky and speculative but they were hearing what they wanted to hear."[5] Meeker engaged in this buck-passing exercise in April 2001, just as America was heading into the recession that economists blamed largely on excessive investment encouraged by the dot.com boom. Be that as it may, the boom threw up evidence aplenty that some brokerages used their analysts to flatter potential clients with rosy research, and worse. Arthur Levitt, the Chairman of the Securities and Exchange Commission, quoted research showing "a direct correlation between the content of an analyst's recommendations and the amount of business his firm does with the issuer."[6]

A few years later after he had left the SEC Levitt made the point more bluntly. "We must better expose Wall Street analysts' conflicts of interest. For years we've known that analysts' compensation is tied to their ability to bring in or support investment banking deals," he told an inquiry into the Enron collapse. "As long as analysts are paid based on banking deals they generate or work on, there will always be a cloud over what they say. Analysts also should not be allowed to trade the stock of any company for which they have issued a recommendation in the last 30 days."[7]

Gibberish and webbygook

Never was the potential for abuse greater than when technology companies came to the stock market in initial public offerings (IPOs). The demand was insatiable and the business profitable. For instance, in the first three months of 2001 alone Goldman Sachs, Morgan Stanley, Merrill Lynch, and Lehman Brothers pulled in nearly $3.5 billion in combined investment banking revenues. The flood of IPOs during the technology boom exposed Chinese walls as flimsy to say the least and sometimes swept them away altogether. IPOs fostered great interdepartmental teamwork, which is admirable at most organizations but unethical when Chinese walls are breached. Too often analysts scouted for privately-owned technology companies which were ripe for a stock market listing and their investment banking colleagues across the Chinese wall then swooped to win the mandate to organize the IPO. Analysts would complete the job by recommending the stock to get the investors drooling. In the atmosphere of the day this teamwork worked well. Analysts who didn't want to play along reported a climate of fear. "[A firm] can't come out bearish on hot groups," said one Wall Street analyst, who refused to be named for fear of jeopardizing his career. "No IPO will come to you if you're recommending selling something in that sector."[8]

A notable exception were analysts Ravi Suria and C. Stan Oh at the Wall Street house Lehman Brothers. In June 2000 they issued a report on Amazon.com's bonds which warned potential investors that the company might run out of cash, saying that it had "the financial characteristics that have driven innumerable retailers to disaster through history." Amid all the hype the report was a breath of fresh air. Barron's, a US business weekly, praised it for dispensing with "the gibberish and webbygook that ooze from virtually all the brokerage stuff churned out on anything tech and everything internet."[9] But Amazon.com's chief, Jeff Bezos, crowned *Time Magazine's* Person of the Year a few months earlier, was less amused and gave Suria and Oh a tongue lashing for the report which clobbered his company's share price.

In the event Amazon didn't run out of cash but the report, issued when Amazon.com shares were worth about $42, offered investors food for thought. By the time the bubble had burst Amazon.com shares had lost about three-quarters of their value. Fund managers loved this kind of honest research as much as chief executives disliked it, something which showed up in a Reuters survey the following year. It surveyed 173 fund managers who managed a total of $5.3 trillion, plus 378 large US corporations. The fund managers voted Lehman Brothers' internet research team of Holly Becker, Harry Blount and Robert Rouse as the best in the industry. The companies, however, disregarded Becker and colleagues entirely.

Perhaps the most controversial aspect of analysts' work is their recommendations to clients which fall roughly into the categories of buy, hold or sell. Here again analysts tend to look on the bright side, issuing a welter of "buy" recommendations but rarely advising anyone to sell anything. Concerns grew so much that questions were raised on Capitol Hill. In 2001 the House of Representatives' capital markets subcommittee held a hearing on the vexed issue. At the hearing Paul Kanjorski, a Pennsylvania Democrat, cited data showing that less than 1 percent of 28,000 recommendations issued by brokerage analysts in late 1999 and most of 2000 advised selling stocks.

For the defence, the President of the Securities Industry Association, Marc Lackritz, pointed out that the Dow Jones Industrial Average and the Standard & Poors 500 index had both risen an average 16 percent a year from 1988 to 1999. In such a bull market analysts would inevitably issue more buy than sell recommendations.

What aggravated investors more than anything else was that some analysts kept issuing buy recommendations even when the market went into free fall in 2000 and 2001. In any case investors with a fixed amount of money have to sell some shares if they want to buy others, a fact of life frequently overlooked by analysts.

Reading between the lines

Inevitably professional investors such as fund managers get wise to such tricks. For instance, a "hold" recommendation often is a polite way of saying "sell." "Part of the skill of the fund manager is to read between the lines, talk to the analyst, talk to the specialist salesman, and work out what the house view really is, rather than what it appears to be," said David Manning, head of British equities at the London-based fund manager Foreign & Colonial. "What you hear on the telephone is not necessarily what you read in the circular."[10]

> **Part of the skill of the fund manager is to read between the lines, talk to the analyst, talk to the specialist salesman, and work out what the house view really is.**

That's fine for the professionals but what about the legions of small investors who take the recommendations at face value, and who can't simply pick up the phone to check them out? One banking group, London-based HSBC, stuck its neck out by requiring its analysts to issue as many "sell" recommendations as "buys," and virtually eliminating "holds." "A 'hold' is just a place for an analyst to hide," said Mark Brown, HSBC's research head at the time.[11] Cynics suggested that HSBC could afford to take such a lofty stance because it was a relatively small player in investment banking and had less to lose by offending clients than its bigger rivals. Such is the industry.

Subject matter is secondary

Economists, who analyze GDP or inflation rather than QXL or Amazon.com, perhaps face fewer conflicts of interest. But the pressure to feed the demand for predictions, be it from market professionals or the public, is equally strong. "An awful lot of people who stand up in front of TV cameras, myself included, are simply doing it for promotional PR reasons, to keep the firm's name in front of the public eye. The subject matter we're talking about is secondary," says Andrew Milligan, head of economic and market analysis at Standard Life Investments.[12]

A few economists achieve the celebrity status that stock analysts enjoy. In the United States, Nobel laureates such as Milton Friedman, the father of monetarist economics, and more recently Joseph Stiglitz, a former chief economist at the World Bank, have become personalities. But outside the United States, economists have to work hard for recognition. In Britain few are likely to be stopped in the street and prodded for a GDP prediction in the same way that US equity analysts dispense stock tips. Nevertheless Britons take a close interest in the state of the economy, as their jobs may depend on it, and particularly in interest rates because most households have borrowed heavily to buy their homes. The demand for economic punditry is therefore large and growing.

Charlie Bean doesn't have to seek that kind of attention. As Chief Economist at the Bank of England, his job is not to sell forecasts but to make them, and act on them as a member of the Bank's Monetary Policy Committee. Bean takes a dim view of his colleagues in the City of London who have to sell themselves and their predictions. City pundits, he says, have two roles: one is producing economic analysis. "But they also have to get publicity for their company by being interviewed on TV or quoted in the newspaper. There is a bit of an incentive there for them to say slightly outrageous things to get noticed," he says.[13]

Economists have, like many other humans, a tendency to congregate in herds. This means they often cluster around the consensus by offering similar predictions to each other. In Britain the consensus figure is often, although not always, close to the "official" forecast produced by the Treasury. There is much to be said for this: if the consensus forecast turns out to be wrong you have the comfort of being in good company. But it is the lone wolves who tend to make themselves heard not only on TV but also with the clients who pay their salaries. "Nobody ever called me up and said 'We would like to interview you, you're saying the same as the Treasury'," says Roy Batchelor at the City University Business School.[14] "There's a market for economic forecasts and if you produce a number there are limited ways you can differentiate your product." One way is to be noticeably more optimistic or pessimistic than the pack. "There are people who may have decided to take a very bullish or very bearish view systematically so that they always stand out from the crowd," says Bean. "People who are quite strong in thinking that inflation will take off get a bit more attention in the press than people who are in the middle of the pack."

> **Economists have, like many other humans, a tendency to congregate in herds.**

The recession that never was

Richard Jeffrey, the former chief economist at Charterhouse Economics, is one of those people who are quite strong in thinking that inflation will take off, and he is indeed a frequent guest on television, radio and in the newspapers. Over the years he has often asserted that the British economy was stronger than his peers, including some at the Bank of England, believed. On occasions he has scolded the Bank for failing to raise interest rates when he thought inflation was heading up. Like everyone, Jeffrey sometimes gets it wrong, but it's the occasions when he is right that everyone remembers. The British recession that never was illustrates this nicely.

In late 1998 the world seemed an insecure place. In the summer Russia had devalued the rouble out of the blue and defaulted on some of its debt. That set off a chain of events that brought down a huge hedge fund called Long-Term Capital Management, a near collapse that threatened to paralyze financial markets around the world. In Britain gloom descended as economists predicted at best a sharp slowdown in growth and quite likely a return to recession – except for Richard Jeffrey, that was. In January 1999 City economists forecast on average in a Reuters poll that the economy would grow a microscopic 0.5 percent that year as a whole, a figure that hid expectations of at least a couple of quarters of contraction. Not for the first time Jeffrey shunned the consensus and entered a forecast of 2.1 percent growth, not much lower than the long-term average for the British economy. In the event he was spot on, the economy grew 2.1 percent in 1999. Of course it takes a lot of luck as well as skill to achieve that kind of accuracy, but reputations can be built on such predictions.

Jeffrey denies that he deliberately distances himself from the consensus but admits it does happen. "If you find yourself outside it can be both a comfortable and an uncomfortable experience. It's always important to be able to explain why you're outside and if things go wrong explain why they have gone wrong. If you happen to be outside the consensus and things go right, that's a pleasurable experience," he says.[15] Jeffrey worked at the London headquarters of ING Barings, an investment bank whose Dutch parent bought Charterhouse in 2000. ING Barings and Charterhouse both produce forecasts of the British economy but they weren't always the same. Jeffrey describes the ING Barings predictions as the mainstream house view while he seemed to accept the role of the lone wolf. "Quite often people will be interested to hear outlying views from somebody they know will argue that view cogently, even if they then discount it," he says. "My view … is a commentary of what is going on in the UK. Rather than being the formal view of the house it is meant to be in some ways provocative."

This idea that economists should stimulate their clients' thought processes rather than merely churning out predictions is not as outlandish as it might seem. Fund managers, who control many billions of dollars of other people's money, are busy people and don't want expensive economists to tell them what they already know. Services like Consensus Economics and Reuters polls already inform them of the consensus view of the market. Often it is precisely the "what if" story that they want to hear, even if they disagree with it. They want to know the odds of various scenarios coming about and to size up the risks they pose to their investments. "[Economists] are paid for saying that's the consensus view but let me tell you a story about why things might evolve a bit differently," says Prakash Loungani at the IMF.[16]

> **This idea that economists should stimulate their clients' thought processes rather than merely churning out predictions is not as outlandish as it might seem.**

So lone wolves are not merely a creation of the media, but in seeking recognition economists may be in league with the media in creating a culture of "short termism." Markets often have a very short-term view of the world. They can react sharply to one month's economic statistic knowing full well that the trend it shows might be reversed the following month. But to react they need a forecast. Andrew Milligan accepts the need for such predictions. "It is an essential oiling of the wheels that people produce short to medium-term forecasts, that the market assimilates them and that the market reacts when events turn out differently to those forecasts," he says.

But fund managers are not traders, hopping in and out of markets by the day. Much of Standard Life's work is investing pension fund money, capital that needs to produce steady returns year-in, year-out so that people can enjoy secure retirements. Therefore Milligan finds the short-term forecasts that pop up in the financial media irritating. Often statistics are dominated by "noise," random movements that give no clue as to what is really happening in the economy. Only by studying longer term trends does this become clear. "It's abundantly clear that the media is simply talking about the day-to-day noise that goes on in the markets … I think we're all falling into a trap of emphasizing the short term," he says. "It's very rare indeed that in the media you see a medium to long-term view and that's partly because these issues are often quite difficult to get to grips with … Understanding some of these trends taking place requires a lot more work on the part of the producer and the listener."

Notes

1 Quoted by Reuters on April 7, 2000.

2 ibid.

3 Quoted by Reuters on August 15, 2000.

4 ibid.

5 Quoted in *Financial Times*, April 16, 2001.

6 Speaking at a meeting of the Securities Industry Association, Boca Raton, Florida, April 13, 1999.

7 Testifying to the Senate Governmental Affairs Committee, January 24, 2002.

8 Quoted in Reuters report, December 17, 1999.

9 Up & Down Wall Street: Virtual Disaster, Barron's, June 24, 2000.

10 Quoted by Reuters, November 1, 2000.

11 Quoted by *Financial Times*, September 3, 2001.

12 Interview with author.

13 Interview with author.

14 Interview with author.

15 Interview with author.

16 Interview with author.

9

The price of rice

"Economists are stupid … We respect what they do but it's their stupidity that they don't respect what we do."

– Alan Shaw, technical analyst at Salomon Smith Barney

"Chartists have no sense of humor."

– Burton Malkiel, Professor of Economics, Princeton University

No form of financial forecasting raises the hackles as much as technical analysis. It has been around at least for many decades, possibly several centuries in one form or other, and yet devotees and doubters of technical analysis still snipe at each other. Sometimes the debate can get personal.

Technical analysts study past patterns of price and volume on markets, usually plotted on graphs, and try to apply them to the future. Because they use graphs, the technicians are also known as chartists. If history doesn't exactly repeat itself, at least it gives strong clues about what is likely to come. The beauty of technical analysis, say its devotees, is that it can be used to predict any market you care to mention, be it for stocks, bonds, currencies or commodities. Likewise the discipline knows no frontiers; it will work as well in Wellington as on Wall Street.

Technical analysis attempts to overcome one of the biggest obstacles to forecasting: human psychology and the apparent tendency of people to behave irrationally. The price of a share or any other security depends on human expectations. If more people expect it to rise than to fall, more people will want to buy the stock than to sell it, and the price will climb. So human behavior determines the change in price and we all know that human behavior can be unpredictable. Technicians therefore scrutinize past patterns on the markets, which themselves were determined by human behavior. Any honest chartist will admit it doesn't

> **Technical analysis attempts to overcome one of the biggest obstacles to forecasting: human psychology and the apparent tendency of people to behave irrationally.**

always work. Humans won't necessarily behave tomorrow as they did yesterday, even in similar circumstances, but a good technician should at least improve the odds of making the right investment.

Technicians sometimes work in windowless rooms; some of them prefer to track prices manually even though computer software for the job abounds. Therefore they need a lot of wall space to post their graphs charting market movements over many years. In any case what goes on in the outside world is of secondary importance. For technical analysts prices matter more than events.

Humanity – at least that part of it engaged in forecasting stocks – can be divided into two tribes: technical analysts who study price and fundamental analysts who study value. The difference is nice but significant. On the stock market a fundamentalist will analyze a company while a technician will analyze the company's share price. A fundamentalist tries to estimate the value of the company by studying its profitability, the quality of its management, its prospects, the economic climate in which it trades and so on. But this, say the technicians, assumes that the value of a company alone determines the price of its share. "In fact price and perceived value are rarely in equilibrium. Prices are set by supply and demand and they represent all that is known, feared and hoped for by the market as a whole and its individual participants," said Bronwin Wood, a fellow of the British Society of Technical Analysts. "Where fundamental analysis focuses on value, technical analysis concerns itself with price, volume of transactions, and individual (and) group psychology."[1]

The Dow Theory

Nothing irritates technicians more than to suggest that fundamental analysis is traditional and their discipline is new-fangled.

Nothing irritates technicians more than to suggest that fundamental analysis is traditional and their discipline is new-fangled. Many believe it is the oldest form of financial analysis in the world. Alan Shaw, the doyen of New York chartists and a pugnacious defender of technical analysis, believes that traders used something similar in seventeenth-century Japan to predict the price of rice. According to Wood the idea also developed separately on the corn markets of England several centuries ago where traders used a system of recording transactions with a series of marks on a page as prices rose and fell. These records helped them to see where supply and demand were in balance, and to decide what price they should agree for future transactions. However, the modern father of technical analysis was Charles Dow, who created what is now the Dow Jones Industrial Average in 1897. From 1900 to 1902 he wrote a series of articles in the *Wall Street Journal* on how the stock market worked which became known as the Dow Theory. Dow used stock market trends as a barometer of general business conditions but most people who subsequently developed his theory concentrated on forecasting share prices themselves.

"I have textbooks and courses that were produced and offered on the subject in 1907," says Shaw, who for decades led technical analysis at what is now the Wall Street house Salomon Smith Barney. In his mid-sixties and semi-retired, Shaw still teaches technical analysis at the New York Institute of Finance. He regularly visits Salomon Smith Barney's chartroom in lower Manhattan, up the street from the ruins of the World Trade Center. Ceiling-to-floor graphs decorate the room, known as "The Laboratory," which is naturally windowless. On one wall is a graph plotting daily market statistics going back to 1982 (the older ones are rolled up in Shaw's office) while the "weekly wall" charts moves back to 1945. "We believe that people used charts way, way back because there were no fundamentals that could be looked at – or if there were they were unreliable or downright lies," says Shaw. "What matters is that technical analysis as an investment decision-making process was around long before accepted fundamental analysis was. So there."[2]

This final retort shows how the rivalry, even hostility between those who love and loathe technical analysis persists a century after Dow wrote his articles. Some economists regard it at best with skepticism and at worst as something akin to astrology. A well-known skeptic is Burton Malkiel, a professor of economics at Princeton University in New Jersey. Malkiel takes a lengthy tilt at the technicians in his book *A Random Walk down Wall Street*.[3] "Some of my best friends are chartists and I have listened very carefully to their explanations but I have yet really to understand them. Indeed many chartists freely admit that *they* don't know why charting should work – history just has a habit of repeating itself," he wrote.

Flipping the coin

Malkiel describes an experiment he conducted with his students. They constructed a chart of a hypothetical stock selling initially at $50 by flipping a coin. If it came up heads they assumed the stock closed the day half a point higher; if it came up tails the price fell half a point. This chart of randomness looked remarkably like a normal stock price chart. "I showed it to a chartist friend of mine who practically jumped out of his skin. 'What is this company?' he exclaimed. 'We've got to buy immediately. This pattern's a classic. There's no question the stock will be up 15 points next week.' He did not respond kindly to me when I told him the chart had been produced by flipping a coin. Chartists have no sense of humor."

In London, economist Richard Jeffrey is likewise suspicious. "When the forecast goes wrong technicians never admit the discipline itself is weak, only the people who practise it," he says. "The technical analyst will always say the chart never lies so therefore it was the interpretation that was wrong." But he admits: "The language of technical analysis is quite seductive, as are some of the statistical techniques."[4]

Seductive or not, the technician's vocabulary is certainly colorful. Tools include bar, point and figure, and candle and swing charts; then there's the Elliott Wave Theory, the Andrews' Pitchfork, Bollinger bands, Japanese candlesticks (they were invented by our seventeenth-century rice traders), Fibonacci arcs, Gann angles and so on. Technicians seek out support and resistance levels, head and shoulders, double tops and triple bottoms. Jeffrey grudgingly accepts that technical analysis sometimes helps for a while, if only because it may produce self-fulfilling prophecies when enough people use it. "There are some markets where you have to under-stand a degree of technical analysis simply because an awful lot of market participants use it," he says. "Currency, interest rate, bond markets will go through periods when technical analysis appears to be quite powerful but in the end those markets are going to be driven by economic fundamentals, and sometimes politics too."

This kind of talk irritates Shaw. "Economists are stupid," he says. "We respect what they do but it's their stupidity that they don't respect what we do. That may be just as well. We don't want them bothering us." Shaw believes economists miss the point. "It's a fact that the fundamentals will eventually prevail but the stock price will already have gone down before the earnings shortfall, or the stock price will have already gone up before [the company] reports the record earnings."

Technicians reject the notion of self-fulfilling prophecies.

Technicians reject the notion of self-fulfilling prophecies. They may all look at the same charts but they won't interpret them identically. Only if they agreed on the interpretation and therefore traded the same way could the forecast move the market. Half a dozen technical

BOX 9.1

·············

A random walk

Mention two phrases to technical analysts and they instantly see red: efficient markets and the random walk. These are theories which suggest it's impossible to predict a financial market, certainly by using charts and possibly by any technique. The Efficient Market Hypothesis emerged from the PhD dissertation of Eugene Farma, now a professor of finance at the University of Chicago. In 1965 Farma published an article entitled *Random Walks in Stock Market Prices*.[1] On efficient markets large numbers of rational people compete to maximize their profits, each trying to predict future prices, he says. Where information is freely available prices at a given moment reflect events that have already occurred and events that the market expects to happen. The efficient market hypothesis has three forms:

- The weak form asserts that all past market prices are reflected in today's price. In other words historic data contains no useful information and technical analysis is a waste of time.

- The semistrong form asserts that all publicly available information is reflected in today's price. Therefore fundamental analysis is a waste of time.

- The strong form asserts that all information is reflected in today's price, so even insider information is of no use.[2]

If I knew that the price of Microsoft or Marks & Spencer shares would rise tomorrow I would buy them today. So would everyone else, given that they have the same information as I do, and the market process would automatically drive up today's price to tomorrow's price. As soon as new information becomes available prices reflect it, assuming that the market can absorb news rapidly. Price movements are due to inherently unpredictable events that aren't already known to the market. According to the random walk theory they don't follow any patterns; past price movements cannot be used to predict future movements. In summary it's impossible to forecast prices or beat the market consistently.

"On Wall Street, the term 'random walk' is an obscenity. It is an epithet coined by the academic world and hurled insultingly at the professional soothsayers," writes Burton Malkiel in his book *A Random Walk Down Wall Street*. "Taken to its logical extreme it means that a blindfolded monkey throwing darts at a newspaper's financial pages could select a portfolio that would do just as well as one carefully selected by the experts."

In the early 1990s the *Wall Street Journal* began a monthly contest pitting the selections of four experts against the selections of four dart throwers. Malkiel threw the darts for the first contest. Over the years the experts seem to have outperformed the dart throwers but hardly conclusively.

1 *Financial Analysts Journal*, September/October, 1965.
2 For a useful summary of the Efficient Markets Hypothesis and the Random Walk Theory go to www.investorhome.com/emh

analysts can look at a chart and produce half a dozen different interpretations but in this respect they're no different from the old enemy. "You show 52 economists the same CPI [consumer price index] report and you get 52 opinions," retorts Shaw. Another myth is that technical analysis alone analyzes the past to predict the future. "Aren't all forms of analysis a look at the past?" A balance sheet is a snapshot of a company's finances on a given day in the past. An economic indicator such as the consumer price index shows only what the inflation rate was in a given month in the past. "Economists look at the past to get a view for the future, and so do we," he says.

Technicians believe in the anticipatory power of stock markets and there is evidence to back them up. Share prices tend to start falling well before economic slowdowns or recessions and begin rising well before an economy picks up. This leads back to the Dow Theory. "He was the first one to make us understand that the stock market was a leading indicator and therefore it's a barometer, not a thermometer. It doesn't tell you what the temperature is, it tells you what the temperature might be," says Shaw. "That's why so often stocks top out when business couldn't be better and bottom out when business couldn't be worse. But lots of people are still very stupid and don't understand that."

A head start

So how does technical analysis work, assuming you believe it does work? Books on the subject could fill a small library but some examples can give a glimpse of the technician's work.

As the technician looks for past patterns to repeat themselves, perhaps what followed the great Japanese stock market bubble of the 1980s can predict what might follow the great American market bubble of the 1990s. The Tokyo bubble burst at the end of 1989 and more than a decade later the Japanese economy has yet to recover, beset by deflation and a banking industry weakened by an accompanying property boom and bust which left it laden with bad debt. America's bubble burst just over 10 years later and even before the attacks of September 11 the threat of recession was plain. Most economists emphasize the differences more than the similarities: while US stock prices became grossly inflated in the late 1990s the same cannot be said for property prices. Likewise the US banking system seems reasonably robust and policymakers, particularly at the Federal Reserve have been nimbler in tackling the threat of recession than were their Japanese counterparts.

But Shaw is not so sure. Salomon Smith Barney has plotted Tokyo's Nikkei 225 stock average starting in 1966 against the Dow Jones Industrial Average starting in 1978. The results are startlingly similar although the fit is better if the Dow is replaced by the Nasdaq Composite index, a measure of US technology stocks, for the final frantic stages of the boom from September 1999 onwards (Figure 9.1).

If the Nikkei graph, which has a 12-year "head start," can indeed predict how the US market is likely to perform in the next few years, investors should be worried. More than a decade after the Japanese bubble burst the Nikkei wallows around 75 percent below its peak value.

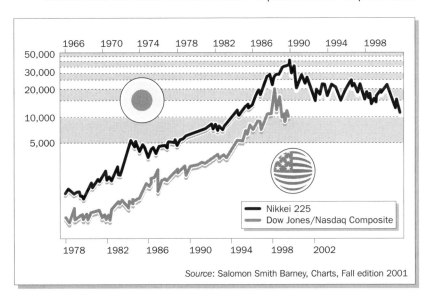

Source: Salomon Smith Barney, Charts, Fall edition 2001

Figure 9.1 *How US stock prices in the bull run 1982–2000 shadowed the Tokyo market's climb more than a decade earlier. Left scale refers to Nikkei average only*

One nuts-and-bolts element of technical analysis is the concept of support and resistance. US technical analyst Steve Achelis explains it this way. "Think of security prices as the result of a head-to-head battle between a bull [the buyer] and a bear [the seller]. The bulls push prices higher and the bears push prices lower. The direction prices actually move reveals who is winning the battle," he said. "Support levels indicate the price where the majority of investors believe that prices will move higher, and resistance levels indicate the price at which a majority of investors feel prices will move lower."[5]

The Dow Jones Industrial Average offers a good example of resistance in the 1970s and early 1980s. Until late 1982 every time it hit the psychological barrier of 1000 the bears would sell and push it back below. But perceptions can change with time and when they do, the change can be abrupt. In late 1982 the Dow staged a breakout at what turned out to be the start of an 18-year bull market, leading to a peak of over 11,700 in January 2000. When resistance is broken it's often a good time to buy (Figure 9.2).

A support level is the opposite: buyers emerge every time a stock, index or whatever slips to a certain level and push it back up. But support levels, like resistance levels, can be breached and when they are it's often a signal to sell.

Support and resistance levels are barriers to change whereas trend analysis is the study of consistent change. A trend, be it rising or falling, can last for years, albeit it with interruptions along the way called corrections. For instance the US stock market, along with many others, suffered big corrections in 1987 and 1998 but they soon recovered and the upward trend lasted from 1982 until 2000. Even for people who aren't interested in the details of technical analysis spotting the trends can be useful. Pinned on the wall of

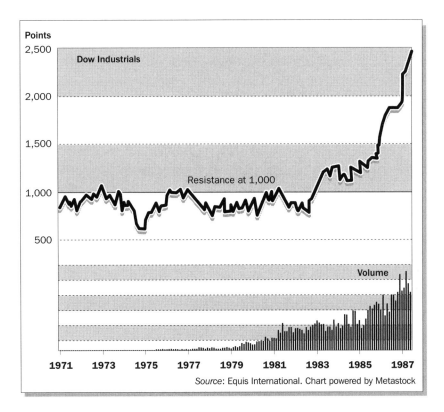

Figure 9.2 *How the Dow Jones Industrial Average*
broke through 1000 points and soared

Salomon Smith Barney's chartroom is a T-shirt with the slogan "The Trend is your Friend." This being after the bubble burst, the words slope downwards. For Shaw this is a more positive version of the old adage "Don't fight the trend." Trendlines can show investors when to stay in a bull market and let the trend carry their investment higher. They can also help investors to cut their losses in a falling market, or prevent bargain hunters from buying too early and getting caught up in the final phase of the decline, which is often the most dramatic. All trends, however long, come to an end and the trick is to distinguish

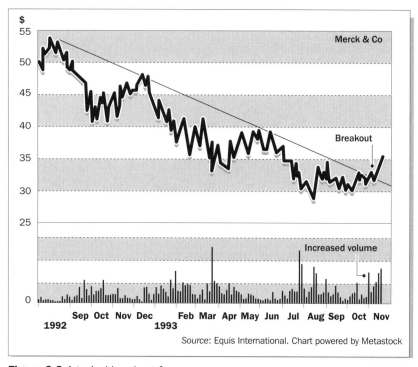

Figure 9.3 *A typical breakout from a long-term trend*

the turning point from the short-term ups and downs of the market. A turning point downwards is a signal to bail out, an upturn a signal to pile into the market. Figure 9.3 shows a typical breakout at the end of a long trend, accompanied by higher volume of transactions – another typical warning signal.

Near the end of trends the pace of change tends to accelerate, both when the market is climbing and falling. For instance, the graph of the Nasdaq composite index rose almost vertically in the final stage of high-tech euphoria in late 1999 and early 2000 (Figure 9.4).

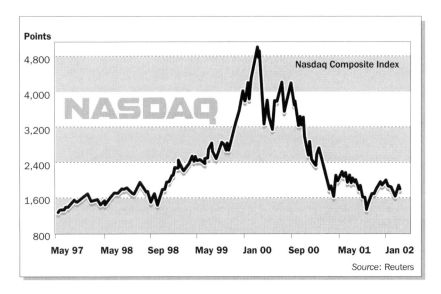

Figure 9.4 *How the Nasdaq Composite succumbed*
to greed and fear

This is known as the "greed" stage when almost everybody throws caution to the wind and piles into the market in the hope of instant riches. The opposite is the "fear" stage when gloom is virtually universal and nearly everyone bails out of the market.

Moving averages, the average level of a stock or index over a given period, are also a popular tool. Investors typically buy when a security's price rises above its moving average and sell when the price falls below. For instance, an analyst wants to plot a 25-day moving average of the Caterpillar stock price. The analyst takes the sum of the closing levels for the last 25 trading days and divides them by 25, and repeats the calculation every day, always using the latest 25 closes. The averages can then be graphed and laid on top of a chart showing daily closing levels. Because it includes data from

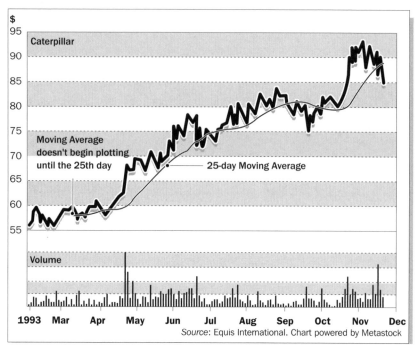

Figure 9.5 *How daily share prices can stray from the moving average*

the past 25 trading days the moving average will always lag the daily movement. If the stock falls below an upward trend in the moving average, this is often a sign of weakness to come. Conversely if it outperforms the moving average in a downward trend, it may be on the way up (Figure 9.5).

Some of the more colorful vocabulary of technical analysis describes the shape of chart patterns. For instance a technician may spot a "head and shoulders" formation at the turning point

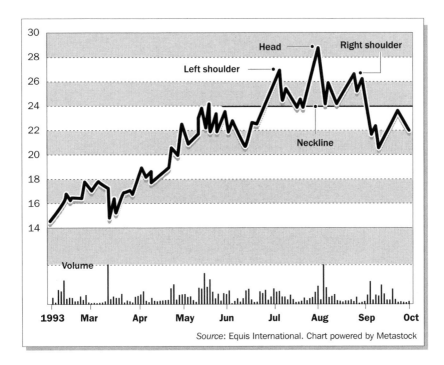

Figure 9.6 *A head and shoulders formation*

from an upward trend to a downward trend. Figure 9.6 shows how such a formation bears a resemblance, albeit passing, to the human anatomy.

When the neckline is penetrated for the second time this is often a sign that the trend has changed from up to down. In a falling market an inverted head and shoulders can form. Other common formations include the double top and double bottom (Figure 9.7).

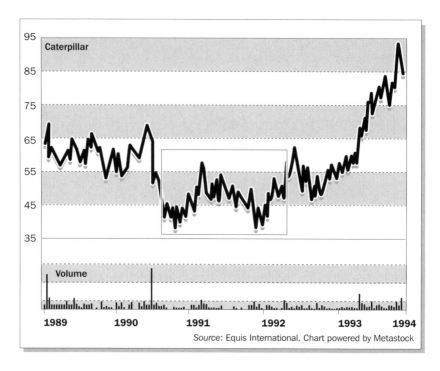

Figure 9.7 *A double bottom*

One thing on which technical analysts and economists do agree is that all markets and economies move in cycles, a series of upward and downward trends which can last from a few weeks to decades. Probably the longest of them all is the long-wave cycle as described by Nikolai Dimitrievich Kondratieff. Louise Yamada, who now leads the technical team at Salomon Smith Barney, tells the story of Kondratieff's rise and fall in a book on technical analysis called *Market Magic*.[6] Kondratieff was a youthful Deputy Minister of Food after the Russian Revolution and drafted the five-year Soviet agricultural plan for Lenin's New Economic Policy. After Lenin's death he turned to academia where he wrote his most influential work, *The Major Economic Cycles*, in 1925. "Kondratieff identified the long-wave economic cycle, suggesting that capitalist economies self-correct and renew; that economic cycles undergo a major rise and fall lasting 48 to 60 years. The rising curve was associated with business expansion, inflation and increasing prosperity; the falling curve with economic contraction, deflation, and a falling standard of living," wrote Yamada.

One thing on which technical analysts and economists do agree is that all markets and economies move in cycles, a series of upward and downward trends which can last from a few weeks to decades.

Any idea that capitalist economies could forever renew themselves did not go down well with Stalin who assumed that capitalism would collapse. So Kondratieff was sent off to Siberia where he died in 1930 well short of his 40th birthday. Only in 1939 did the economist Joseph Schumpeter return to the theory, describing the waves as "gales of creative destruction" as new industries swept away the old and new technology fuelled an upswing. In modern history the waves have been triggered by steam power, which drove the industrial revolution (1780s–1840s), the railway age (1840s–1890s), the arrival of electric power (1890s–1930s), the motor vehicle (1930s–1980s) and the present information and communications revolution which began in the 1980s (Figure 9.8).

What does this all mean for the stock market? According to Yamada, since the end of the 19th century a long-term bull and bear cycle on Wall Street has accompanied each of the long wave economic cycles. Sometimes they have been out of step but for

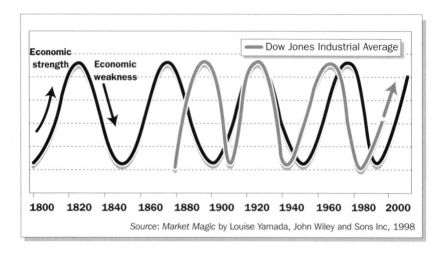

Figure 9.8 *The Kondratieff Cycle*

instance the US stock market's bull market from 1982 to 2000 parallels the information revolution and development of its primary tool, the personal computer. In other words the work of an obscure Soviet economist may signal long-term trends on that most capitalist of institutions, the stock market.

The other side of the demographic mountain

Technical analysts, like other analysts and economists, spread their net widely when they seek reasons for long-term market trends. In recent decades that net has fallen on demographic change. Human behavior affects markets and what changes our behavior more than the aging process? Young people tend to spend rather than save because they think less about preparing for the future and more about enjoying the present. Partying tends to take priority over pensions. But as we enter middle age reality dawns that we must think about retirement. Reluctantly we cut down on nights out and start saving for the future. Much of those savings find their way into the stock market, either directly or through pension funds.

There's nothing new about growing up but what is changing is the demographic makeup of the wealthy nations, where most of the saving is done. After World War Two the birth rate climbed steadily, reaching a peak in the United States and many other western nations in the late 1950s. The "baby boomers" did their partying in the 1970s and 1980s but by the 1990s they had reached middle age and were starting to save, largely by buying stocks. This is a powerful argument when trying to explain why stock markets rose so strongly in the last years of the 20th century, say many technical analysts. But this demographic buying of stocks cannot last for ever: after retirement the baby boomers will stop saving as their income from work dries up and start living off their savings, largely by selling their investments. An aging population may not be good for the Dow Jones Industrial Average.

Here, once again, Japan may offer clues to the future. In *Market Magic* Yamada argues that it may "reflect the other side of the demographic mountain." Japan has one of the oldest populations in the industrial world and by 2025 more than a quarter of its people will be over 65. In demographic terms Japan is about a decade ahead of the United States. Could this help to explain why Japanese stocks peaked at the end of 1989 and the US market 10 years later, give or take a few months? Yamada's book, however, appeared in 1998 when euphoria was sweeping US stocks ever higher. She, like so many others, failed to predict that the end was so close. She wrote: "There will come, we can be sure, an eventual end to this cycle of US financial inflation. But the demographic studies suggest that may not begin until 2004–2010 when the front end of the baby boomers will begin to retire, or further to 2014, when, at age 68 they are calculated to cease acquiring financial assets. There should be at least a decade of continued savings inflow until the bulk of the baby boomers achieve retirement age – at which point money should slowly withdraw from equities and financial asset savings vehicles, including retirement funds and pensions. These demographic influences on the movements of money may then see the stock market slowly drift back to its uninflated value levels."

Big deal

With the benefit of hindsight this suggests that technical analysts can miss the great turning points as much as any other forecaster. Yamada stands her ground, blaming high-technology hysteria for speeding up the process. "Theoretically we were looking for the top demographically to come into place [in] 2004–2010. Well the bear doesn't wait till he's invited to tea," she says. "That speculative excess brought it to an end sooner; a couple of years early. Big deal."[7]

For anyone who went into stocks, confident that demographics would protect their investment well into the 21st century, the dramatic turn of 2000–2001 must indeed have been a big deal. Yamada's answer is blunt. "I don't think one should be actively in the market today. I think one should be actively in preservation of capital mode," she says. Technical analysis cannot predict when a bubble will burst any more than other forecasting techniques; it can only warn investors that they're treading on thin ice.

One way of protecting your capital is to quit stocks and put the money into something safe, such as US treasury bonds. Shaw says 80 percent of his personal investments are in bonds, with the remaining 20 percent in stocks. Nevertheless Smith Barney Mutual Funds announced in September 2000, as the Nasdaq bubble was deflating and the wider market was close to its peak, that it had launched a fund using the work of the technical research team. The Smith Barney Group Spectrum Fund uses a model based on technical analysis to invest in the stock market sectors which offer the best opportunity to outperform the Standard & Poor's 500 index.

So how do the technicians at Salomon Smith Barney see the future, now that the bubble has burst? The optimism of 1998 has vanished, to be replaced by an alarming degree of gloom. "It looks uncomfortably like 1929," says Yamada. In the Wall Street crash the Dow Jones Industrial Average fell no less than 89 percent, sucking the US economy into a deflationary spiral and the Depression. Yamada now believes a structural bear market has returned. That doesn't mean a relatively brief downward blip, as in 1987 and 1998, but rather a long-term fall in share prices. How long is long term? "Maybe you should start looking for a bottom somewhere about 2015 or 2012, but nothing is etched in stone," she says. Wall Street took more than 12 years to start recovering from the crash of 1929. The 20th century's other structural bear market lasted even longer, from 1966 to 1982. This time the market didn't fall so spectacularly but it was an era of high inflation which ate into the real value of shares. Adjusted for inflation the Dow lost 75 percent of its value.

The long-term average growth rate of the US stock market is about 7 percent a year. In the late 1990s it was triple that but economic theory suggests that growth rates must, sooner or later, return to the average. "Never in market history in the United States have we had five consecutive years of 20 percent or more. So how do we get back to the average of plus seven?" says Shaw. The answer is at best a period of stagnation, at worst a sharp drop in prices. "One of the reasons why we're in a structural bear market now is because we were for 20 years in a structural bull market. That's not very difficult to understand but some people don't want to understand that," he says.

The Yamada–Shaw view is startlingly pessimistic compared with that of their antagonists, the economists. Given that US recessions have averaged 11 months since World War Two company earnings ought to recover in due course and, if you believe in the anticipatory power of the stock market, share prices should pick up even sooner.

Yamada was speaking less than a couple of months after the attack on the World Trade Center. But technicians believe that events outside their windowless offices, even those as shocking as September 11, merely modify pre-ordained market trends. The stock market paused only briefly in 1963 when President John F. Kennedy was assassinated because it was on a bull run. The story, says Yamada, is much the same for the September 11 disaster except in reverse: this time the market had just embarked on a bear trend. "September 11 was nothing more than a compression of time and price of something that would have happened over the next six months anyway," she says.

At the end of January 2002 the Dow was more than 300 points *higher* than it closed the day before the attack. On financial markets anything can happen but so far the bear seems to be reluctant to come to tea.

Notes

1 *What is Technical Analysis?* By Bronwin Wood. This is a brief introduction available on the website of the Society of Technical Analysts at www.sta-uk.org/bw_wita.pdf

2 Interview with author.

3 *A Random Walk Down Wall Street*, W.W. Norton and Co, revised edition published 1999.

4 Interview with author.

5 *Technical Analysis from A to Z*, by Steven B. Achelis, McGraw-Hill, second edition 2001. This material is also available online at www.equis.com/free/taaz/inttechnicalanalysis.html

6 *Market Magic* by Louise Yamada, John Wiley and Sons Inc, 1998.

7 Interview with author.

10

Doctor Doom

"Most wealth has been created and then destroyed again ... Most companies fail, most countries fail over time, cities come up and then they go down. You just have a lot of accidents."

– Marc Faber, alias Doctor Doom

Pessimists tend to be scarce when stock markets boom. During the 1990s optimists dominated the financial press and business TV, many of them predicting that companies' profits, and their share prices, could rise almost indefinitely. But a small band of forecasters swam against the tide, warning investors of a speculative bubble that was sure to burst – some time. Those who attracted the most media attention, willingly or otherwise, were nicknamed "Doctor Doom." This chapter looks at two prominent pessimists who had little in common beyond a conviction that the more stock prices inflated, the greater the shock would be when the bubble

Pessimists tend to be scarce when stock markets boom.

inevitably burst. One came from the traditionally discreet business of pension fund management and says he loathed life in the media spotlight; the other is a professional pundit who lives on publicity. Both knew the market would crash but neither knew when.

Tony Dye and the theory of reverse Darwinism

"In bubbles you get a kind of reverse Darwinism – survival of the stupidest," says Tony Dye. "If you're not optimistic and you're realistic you get the sack." Dye, once one of Britain's top pension fund managers, spotted the great stock market bubble of the late 1990s five years before it burst. But far from making him a hero, this forecast earned him a grilling by the media, which nicknamed him Doctor Doom, and eventually cost him his job. Convinced that high-tech "glamour" stocks would collapse, he shunned the sector while it rocketed. In some cases he withdrew completely from the US stock market, the world's biggest. While Dye swam against the tide many of his rivals swam with it, producing spectacular profits for several years. His company, Phillips and Drew Fund Management (PDFM), slid from the top of the performance league tables to the bottom and customers walked out with billions of pounds in investments in search of better returns elsewhere. Finally Dye was squeezed out of PDFM only a few days before New York's Nasdaq share market, the home of high-tech mania, began to collapse. In financial forecasting timing is crucial and while Dye was sure the boom would end, he had little idea when it would end. Time proved him right, but by then it was too late.

Fund management is a huge industry, particularly in the United States, Japan and Britain. Pension funds own about 20 percent of all stocks on the London Stock Exchange. The value of their investments naturally rises and falls with the markets but at the end of 1999 British pension funds held global assets worth $1.3 trillion. The figure for Japanese funds was $1.5 trillion and for US funds $7.7 trillion. The men and women who manage these sums tread a fine line: they must produce a good return on the investment without taking excessive risks with the life savings of pensioners, present and future. League tables track their performance against each other and against the main stock market indices, such as the Standard & Poor's 500 in New York and the FTSE 100 in London. Those that head the tables demand rich rewards. In good times a top British fund manager can easily take home £1 million a year in basic salary and bonus.

Fund management is a huge industry, particularly in the United States, Japan and Britain.

Tony Dye joined this world in 1969 after graduating from the London School of Economics. He was no product of the stockbroker belt, the leafy suburbia surrounding London, but of the northern industrial city of Sheffield. Over the years Dye worked his way up to one of the top jobs in the industry, chief investment officer at Phillips and Drew. He built a reputation as one of the canniest fund managers in the City of London, for instance pulling out of Japanese stocks well before they headed into a slump in 1989. Dye became a leading exponent of "value investment", a strategy which made legendary Wall Street investor Warren Buffett one of America's richest men. Value investors seek out companies which are unfashionable but offer good prospects of profit growth. While everyone else piles into fashionable companies, inflating their stock price, the value investor quietly buys cheap shares in firms which have been overlooked by analysts, the media and the rest of the stock market hype machine. If all goes to plan the unfashionable companies produce some good earnings, become fashionable and their share price climbs, allowing the value investor to walk away with a handsome profit.

Dye's dash for cash

Dye made a good living this way but lived relatively modestly and remained little known outside the City at a time when other high-flyers displayed their wealth ostentatiously. His life, however, changed for good in early 1995 when he decided that stock markets, particularly in the United States, were overheating. The profits that many companies were making, and were likely to make, no longer justified the high price of their shares. "The bubble started developing then. All the tried and tested valuation methods started to be beaten at that stage," he said. "If you believe in valuations, once they're too high you really don't feel like playing very much."[1]

Reluctant to play along with inflating an equity bubble, Dye simply banked 15 percent or more of the £60 billion that PDFM managed. Cash is safe and deposit interest rates can offer the best returns on an investment when stock markets are falling. But stock markets were not falling at the time. Far from it, they were enjoying their biggest boom since World War Two. Dye stuck to his guns but the markets kept on rising, notwithstanding some short-lived reversals such as in the summer of 1998. Between the start of 1995 and the start of 2000 the Dow Jones Industrial Average rose more than 200 percent and the Nasdaq Composite Index, home to many of the hottest technology stocks, gained a staggering 570 percent. PDFM, owned by the Swiss bank UBS, naturally missed out on this boom and began to slide down the league tables, testing the patience of its clients. In 1998 its flagship Phillips and Drew UK Exempt Fund, which alone managed £1.13 billion, made a return of 9.4 percent. Normally that would be an excellent performance and more than enough to keep pensioners well provided for. But 1998 was no normal year on the stock markets and nearly everyone else did much better: the fund was ranked 57 out of 64 in a survey by pension fund consultancy Combined Actuarial Performance Services (CAPS). Its performance over three years was even worse, putting it third from bottom of the league table, a humiliation for one of the great names in British fund management. Phillips and Drew issued a statement regretting "our poor performance" but stood by Dye's strategy even though it had raised many eyebrows.

At the end of 1998 the fund held no stocks whatsoever in the United States, which accounts for more than half the total value of global stock markets. Strikingly 17.8 percent of the fund was held in cash. Usually fund managers keep their cash quota well in single figures, particularly when share prices are rising strongly. After all, anyone can put their money in the bank and earn modest rates of interest, so why pay a top fund management company high fees to do it for you? Fund managers earn their salaries by outperforming cash, and where better to do this than on a stock market that was enjoying its longest bull run in history? Fed up with the poor performance, clients quit PDFM in droves.

Dye, however, began to feel the heat earlier than this and much of it came from the media. Strictly speaking, Dye is no Market Prophet. All his forecasts remained in house and, unlike many forecasters who court publicity, Dye says he found celebrity status deeply unwelcome. Years later he can name a single newspaper article which began a media grilling that lasted four years. Headlined "Dash for cash puts Dye on the spot," the report appeared in the *Sunday Telegraph* on September 15, 1996. The timing was unfortunate. British media had just developed an interest in the usually arcane world of fund management because of a scandal at another venerable name in the business, Morgan Grenfell Asset Management. Morgan Grenfell's star fund manager Peter Young and others were accused of siphoning off millions of pounds to invest in the kind of high-tech, high-risk stocks that Dye wouldn't touch. Young only whetted the tabloids' appetite by turning up to court wearing high heels and a dress. He was eventually ruled unfit to stand trial on grounds of insanity. No one was ever convicted in the case.

Illogical though it may seem, the media likened this fraud case to Dye's decision to leave money in the bank. "The whole press went mad. They thought they had another Peter Young," recalls Dye. "It was horrific really. My face was over every national newspaper ... It was everywhere. Every-bloody-where. Then it was in the open. If the market went up it was easy. I was an easy piece of shit to kick."

Repealing the law of gravity

Rather than dodging the media attention, Dye gave interviews defending his strategy and wrote newspaper columns arguing in detail why stocks were heading for a crash. In one article he cited price/earnings ratios, a common way of valuing stocks by comparing their price with the earnings per share of the company. These showed that US stocks were three times as expensive when compared with company earnings than at the bottom of the previous bear market in 1982. "Has the law of gravity been repealed? The answer must be no," he wrote. "It is almost impossible to overestimate the power of psychology on investors – both retail and institutional. Pressure to conform to the market's view results in capitulation as institutional investors buy shares because of fear of short-term underperformance. Retail investors get carried away with the prospect of 'easy money.' Fear and greed abound. As was said in the 1930s, after the 1929 crash, 'the greater the craze the higher the level of intellect that succumbs to it.' In the end, however, the process exhausts itself as every last bull is fully invested and the last capitulator has capitulated. It is this process, rather than any major news event, that turns the market."[2]

Few people would argue with this analysis now but in 1997 there were plenty who did. Many people in the industry, however, admired Dye's courage in pursuing a low risk strategy for his clients at such a high risk to his own career. Neither was he alone. For instance, Gartmore Investment Management, a fund manager belonging to NatWest Bank, also raised its cash holdings to 17 percent around that time. But for some people Dye almost became a figure of fun. *Management Today* magazine put him second on its list of "Ten people you are glad you weren't in 1997." "Dye comes with a formidable reputation and has commented that he is prepared to wait as long as it takes for a market crash; whether his clients are as patient is another matter," it said.[3]

The end of the road came in March 2000. PDFM admitted that clients had withdrawn about £8 billion from the group in the previous year alone. Altogether 47 clients had left entirely while others had moved part of their funds to rival managers. UBS decided to merge PDFM with its Chicago-based fund management unit run by another big figure in the industry, Gary Brinson. UBS stood by the value investment strategy but the new structure had room for neither Dye nor Brinson. By early March, Dye had gone fishing in the Bahamas to contemplate his future. Within days, on March 10, 2000 to be precise, the Nasdaq Composite hit a record high of 5048 points and immediately began one of the steepest dives in stock market history, tumbling 60 percent in the following 12 months. Dye had been right – eventually.

> **The Nasdaq Composite hit a record high and immediately began one of the steepest dives in stock market history.**

Dye insists he was not fired, but admits to making mistakes, up to a point. "In terms of perceptions I was obviously much too early and that was a fundamental mistake. In terms of doing what you think is sensible and maintaining your principles, I did everything right," he says. When the US market tumbled it pulled with it many of the fund managers who had played along. In the short term the Dye strategy had failed but in the longer term it began to pay off as some of the funds he had once overseen shot back up the league tables.

Greenspan: one of the worst Fed chairmen?

Mention bubbles and the Dye hackles naturally rise. "Everybody just loves a stock market bubble. Instant riches are what people are buying but it's fantastic greed that drives the economy in a way that makes the politicians look good," says Dye. "It's difficult for the politicians to want to stop it. It's very, very unpopular to say anything negative about it. The opposition can't say this is runaway nonsense, so there's a tremendous responsibility on the central bank." Dye feels that the US central bank, the Federal Reserve, and its chairman Alan Greenspan failed to meet that responsibility. By December 1996 Greenspan already seemed worried about the steep climb in stock prices. In comments which briefly jolted markets he warned investors of the dangers of "irrational exuberance" and the possibility that the US stock market might suffer an unexpected and prolonged contraction like in Japan. To many Greenspan is the master of monetary policy, decisively cutting interest rates to restore confidence during the hedge fund crisis of 1998. But to Dye these rate cuts merely pumped money into the economy which funded the wild stock market speculation the following year. "History will measure Mr Greenspan as probably one of the worst ever chairmen of the Federal Reserve board. He allowed a bubble to happen even though he probably had an inkling of it himself when he talked about irrational exuberance. But then in the end he started to become the spokesperson of all this crap about new technology and productivity," says Dye.

Dye's opinion of fellow fund managers who joined the mania is little better. "There are two types of people who were playing the market at this time. There were those who actually believed this nonsense and probably still believe it; they think we're just having an interim period before it all comes back again," he says. "Then there are people who didn't really believe it but just went with the flow. They thought they could see when everybody else was about to get out and jump out ahead of them – which one in a million does."

Today Dye has exchanged a £60 billion world of pension funds for a 23 million euro hedge fund, appropriately called the Contra Fund, which he runs with another refugee from the pensions business, Ed Knox. But he denies feeling frustrated that the market turned his way just as he left PDFM. "I was really pleased," he says. "From looking an absolute idiot suddenly you're resurrected as someone who was quite shrewd. That's got to be good for anybody."

Marc Faber and the tale of a ponytail

More than a decade ago Marc Faber bet that the Japanese stock market would fall at least 50 percent and promised that when it did, he would cut off his trademark ponytail. Today Faber still has the ponytail but only because he failed to keep the promise: the Nikkei stock average, which peaked at 38,915 points at the end of 1989, fulfilled his forecast little more than two years later and kept on falling. By September 2001 it was down 75 percent.

Faber makes his living as a prophet of doom although, he insists, predicting which market will collapse next is not his sole source of income. A Swiss who has lived in the Far East for almost 30 years, he earned the title of Doctor Doom by forecasting the global stock market crash of October 1987 a week before it happened. Then he built a career in spotting bubbles from Japan and southeast Asia to Latin America and the United States. Anyone who followed his advice may have made a lot of money but, he admits, may also have lost a lot. For detecting bubbles is relatively easy; forecasting when they will burst is just about impossible.

Faber, whose clipped Swiss German accent somehow complements the slightly sinister aura of a doomster, has been a
contrarian for most of his career. After finishing his studies in 1970
(his real doctorate comes from the
London School of Economics) he joined
a US firm which sent him to Hong Kong
in 1973. Five years later the Wall Street
investment bank Drexel Burnham
Lambert hired him to set up an Asian
office in Hong Kong. Drexel Burnham
and one of its executives Michael Milken symbolized all that was
excessive on Wall Street in the 1980s. Milken built an empire
based on junk bonds, debt offering high yields but also high risk
and low credit ratings, which financed a wave of huge "leveraged
buyouts" (LBOs). Investors with little reputation or track record
launched audacious bids to take over some of America's biggest
corporations and needed billions of dollars to do so. Mike Milken
obliged, arranging junk bond issues and selling them, often to
unsuspecting savings and loans institutions (S&Ls), the rough US
equivalent of British building societies. It was at this time, while
Milken was on course to becoming America's richest man, that
Faber spotted a crash in the making and it nearly cost him his job.
"In the mid-1980s I started to write very negative reports about the
junk bond market and I almost got sacked," he says. "Mike Milken
started to travel in the Far East and his salesmen tried to peddle
junk bonds to every institution the way they had peddled them to
S&Ls in America. I would go round and say 'don't touch this
garbage.' I had been an early buyer of junk bonds in the 1970s
when they were very depressed and offered some good value. But
in the mid-1980s there was this LBO mania and it had gone to

> **Detecting bubbles is relatively easy; forecasting when they will burst is just about impossible.**

excess. I recognized that and they were really pissed off."[4] In 1990 Milken's junk bond empire, in reality a house of cards, collapsed and he went to jail for two years. Together the bank and the man paid $1.3 billion to settle an array of civil law suits.

Faber picked up the pieces of Drexel Burnham in Hong Kong and went into punditry. In October 1987 he published two very negative commentaries on the stock market, and the stock market obliged by crashing all round the world. On October 19 the Dow dived 22.6 percent, far outstripping a 12.8 percent tumble on the worst day of the Wall Street crash. The chairman of the Hong Kong Stock Exchange Ronald Li (who also ended up in jail) panicked and closed the market for four days. When it reopened on October 26 the Hang Seng Index tumbled 33 percent in one day. Faber would for ever be Doctor Doom.

A couple of years later, not for the only time, Faber found himself playing Cassandra again. "Then came the Japanese bubble and in 1989 I became very negative about Japanese stocks," he says. "I made several bets that the market would fall a minimum 50 percent from its high. Of course nobody believed me and then it happened." Why did the ponytail stay? Faber pleads that having lost half his hair to the aging process he didn't feel like chopping any more off.

Faber's next two prophecies on Asia and the United States likewise proved correct but also underline the biggest problem for the professional doomster, getting the timing right. In 1994 he turned negative on Asian nations, which at the time were amongst the fastest growing in the world, but their stock markets, currencies and economies did not start to collapse for another three years. At a "Bulls versus Bears" debate he forecast that Hong Kong property prices would plunge 50 percent, taking with them the Hang Seng stock index, which was at 9500 points at the time. "It can go to 3000 or 6000 or anywhere in that range," he said. "In 12, 18, 24 months from now it will be significantly lower."[5] Twelve months later the index was lower, but hardly significantly lower, at 9400 and two years later it had jumped to over 11,000. Indeed it reached more than 16,000 before the Asian crash began in 1997.

A costly proposition

On the United States, Faber had this to say: "I think the US stock market will be the next bubble to burst ... I recommend shorting the US technology sector, particularly internet-related stocks which suffer from a tremendous overvaluation."[6] Short selling in a falling market can be immensely profitable. An investor borrows stocks and sells them at a high price in anticipation of a sharp fall in their value. After the fall the investor buys the stocks back cheaply, returns them to the owner and pockets the difference. The bigger the fall, the bigger the profit. If Faber had given this tip in the spring of 2000, when the Nasdaq Composite index began its 60 percent plunge in 12 months, anyone who followed his advice would have become rich. Sadly he didn't. The recommendation dates from July 1996 when the Nasdaq Composite was around 1100, almost 4000 points below its peak four years later. For a short-seller the more the market rises, the greater is the loss (Figure 10.1).

"I'm the first one to admit that we made a lot of bad calls," says Faber. "If you recommended selling short the Nasdaq in 1996 then it's a costly proposition. Why did the Nasdaq peak out at 5000 and

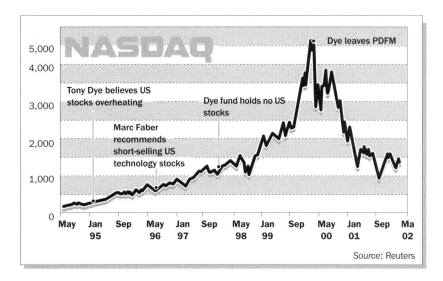

Figure 10.1 *Like comedy, it's all about timing. Tony Dye and Marc Faber's record of timing measured against the Nasdaq Composite Index*

not at 4000 or 6000? There's no reason for it. It's a coincidence, it could have gone on for another three months, it could have burst three months earlier. These are things you just don't know. A bubble is a bubble."

Gold, for many years a Faber favorite, provides another lesson in the need for precise timing. At the end of the 1970s the Soviet Union invaded Afghanistan, one of the tensest moments of the Cold War. "Between the end of 1979 and January 1980 the gold price doubled and the silver price more than doubled before it collapsed. If you had told your clients to sell short, by being off by one

Gold provides another lesson in the need for precise timing.

month you would maybe have been wiped out," says Faber. Perhaps a little late in the day he says that before acting on any forecast the investor needs to ask one question: what is the loss if I'm wrong? Following some forecasts involves somewhat less risk than short selling US technology shares in 1996. For instance Faber forecast in 1998 that the Hong Kong dollar's fixed exchange rate with the US dollar, imposed in 1983, could not last.

Speculators indeed attacked the peg of HK$7.8 to the US dollar during the Asian crisis in the late 1990s but the Hong Kong government fought them off. This prediction has therefore proved to be wrong, at least so far, but need not have involved a heavy loss. A speculator could buy a put option on the Hong Kong dollar, in essence a bet that the currency will fall, relatively cheaply from a bank. If the peg held the option would expire unused and the speculator would lose only the relatively modest premium he had to pay the bank. But if the peg snapped and the Hong Kong dollar fell the speculator could exercise the option and make a big profit. "It's a very low risk bet to implement," says Faber.

Right or wrong, Faber's forecasts sell well. There is a demand for contrarian thinking and he likes satisfying it. "In a way I enjoy it. The investment community was just so naively bullish all the time. Especially in the last few years they believed that stocks always went up whereas the historical evidence is totally against that," he says. One colleague in the 1980s was Abby Joseph Cohen, who became one of Wall Street's most influential gurus during the technology mania. "If someone is always bullish and there happens to be an 18-year bull market, then of course that person becomes famous like Abby Cohen. But it can be that afterwards there is a 10-year bear market and these people are totally discredited because they're always bullish," says Faber. "Abby Cohen was at Drexel Burnham when I was there. She was bullish, bullish, bullish, she didn't see the crash coming in 1987 and especially she didn't see that Drexel would go bankrupt."

Investing in the Helmsman

For many years Faber made much of his income in Hong Kong from managing investments for a group of wealthy clients. But that business dwindled as some of the aging clients died and others retired to Europe just as costs in Hong Kong, particularly for office space, were going through the roof. So Faber bought a compound in the Thai city of Chiang Mai and built a traditional-style home along with an office and library. There he also keeps one of his more unusual investments, a stockpile of memorabilia glorifying the founder of communist China, Mao Zedong. He began buying the stash, including thousands of badges plus posters and porcelain busts of the Great Helmsman, in the 1970s, long before Mao memorabilia became trendy. Faber loves the exotic, none more so than his investment in North Korean debt. Although one of the most reclusive states in the world, North Korea briefly emerged in the 1980s to borrow $800 million from western banks. Needless to say it defaulted on the loans a few years later but the debt still traded with its value rising and falling, depending on whether investors thought the money would ever be repaid. Faber says he bought the debt in the early 1990s at between 10 and 15 cents for every dollar owed, and sold it for 55 to 60 cents in 1996–7. Investors are still waiting for their money back.

Naturally such stories attract media attention which Faber needs because these days punditry earns much of his daily bread. He publishes a newsletter, the *Gloom, Boom and Doom Report* (Tony Dye, incidentally, is a subscriber) and writes magazine columns in English and German. In Asia he is widely known because of commentaries he writes for Chinese-language newspapers in Hong Kong, Taiwan and Malaysia, and speaking at investment conferences is also well-paid work; all of which reinforces his reputation as Doctor Doom, even though he says this is not entirely fair. "People who know me, the professionals, know that I also have bullish forecasts but it is true that the man in the street knows me for the bearish forecasts, which is to some extent unfair but I don't care. In this business it doesn't matter how, as long as you are well known you get better paid," he says. Fair or unfair, Faber cannot resist laying on the gloom. "Most wealth has been created and then destroyed again," he says. "Most companies fail, most countries fail over time, cities come up and then they go down. You just have a lot of accidents."

Notes

1 Interview with author.

2 Article by Dye in the *Daily Telegraph*, August 18, 1997.

3 Ten people you're glad you weren't ... in 1997, *Management Today*, December 1997.

4 Interview with author.

5 Quoted by Reuters, May 31, 1994.

6 Quoted by the *South China Morning Post*, July 14, 1996.

11

Terminator technology

"There is no scope for human bias to get in the way of a good decision."

– David Jubb, Standard Life Investments

Behind a neo-classical façade in Edinburgh, a hospital manager called Harry Smith has created a computer that can learn from experience, a "black box" that eschews human emotions to predict financial markets. A world away from the damp Scottish capital in Santa Fe, New Mexico, the country is arid and the façades are Spanish colonial style. But there a team of physicists – co-led by a former researcher from Los Alamos, the home of the atom bomb – also builds computer systems which predict and play the US stock market. Both Smith and the Santa Fe team use artificial intelligence, albeit in different ways, to prevent human bias from getting in the way of a good investment decision. That, at least, is the theory.

Black boxes are not uncommon on financial markets, but the degree of science they use varies from conventional mathematics to theories at the frontiers of knowledge which have little or no record of reliability. Indeed definitions of what constitutes a black box vary. Some people apply the term loosely to almost any computer forecasting or trading system, provided there's an element of mystery about how it works; others believe a black box must use artificial intelligence (AI) to qualify. Certainly the contents of many black boxes are often comprehensible only to a few academics who have built them; when they use AI usually even the scientists have little idea of what's going on inside. Hedge funds, private investment pools for financial institutions and very wealthy people, often use black boxes and none has done more to besmirch their good name than Long-Term Capital Management. For four years LTCM, a hedge fund run by an elite band of Wall Street bond traders plus a couple of Nobel economics laureates, used computer systems in a seemingly brilliant but ultimately disastrous investment strategy. LTCM's near collapse in 1998 threatened to paralyze financial markets and forced Wall Street and the US Federal Reserve into emergency action. It's debatable whether LTCM's computer systems were black boxes at all because they used conventional, albeit complex, mathematics. Nevertheless the fiasco reinforced the skepticism of those people who doubt that computers can ever forecast or trade the markets better than humans.

> **Black boxes are not uncommon on financial markets, but the degree of science they use varies from conventional mathematics to theories at the frontiers of knowledge.**

Black boxes are used to predict and trade anything from stocks and bonds to currencies and oil. Typically they are computer programs which digest huge amounts of data, particularly historic and current market prices plus the volume of transactions, and spit out a forecast or a recommendation of what to buy or sell, and when. Some systems go further by trading automatically with little or no human intervention. "Conventional" black boxes rely on the same mathematical formulae until a human decides to change them. As in life, however, circumstances change on financial markets and data on past events fed to the computer may no longer be a reliable guide to the future. Systems using some forms of AI go a step further: they adapt to new circumstances by changing the formulae themselves. This kind of black box tries to learn from experience just as humans do, albeit not always successfully.

Black boxes are used to predict and trade anything from stocks and bonds to currencies and oil.

AI can trace its roots back to research in the 1940s and in the early days British academic Alan Turing devised a test of computer intelligence. Turing is popularly known for his work in breaking coded messages sent to and from German submarines in World War Two using Enigma machines. But he was also a pioneer of computer science and in 1950 published a paper describing what is now called the Turing Test. In this game someone would put questions, via text messages, to a computer and a human being in separate rooms. If the questioner could not tell from the answers which was which, it would be fair to call the computer intelligent. However, the term artificial intelligence was not coined until six years later. It emerged from a workshop at Dartmouth College in the US state of New Hampshire when scientists discussed what machines could and might do in the future. Many people have tried to define AI. In 1978 the late mathematician Richard Bellman, a professor at the University of Southern California, summed up what is now a large and varied field of science as "the automation of activities that we associate with human thinking, activities such as decision-making, problem solving, learning."[1]

A Space Odyssey

AI has found a home in Hollywood, particularly since the psychopathic computer HAL starred in Stanley Kubrick's 1969 movie *2001: A Space Odyssey*. Director Steven Spielberg took over another Kubrick idea, unrealized when he died in 1999, and turned it into a film simply called *AI Artificial Intelligence*. This is the story of a boy robot called David who (or perhaps which) is programed to love. But probably Hollywood's best-known AI character – albeit a less loving   one – is The Terminator, a gun-toting robot played by Arnold Schwarzenegger. The Terminator learns human behavior from an artificial neural network, an AI tool which seeks to mimic the brain. Science fiction this may be but AI is also science fact and not just on financial markets. In fact AI is better established outside the markets: computers which play chess against humans use AI, as do supermarkets to forecast demand for their products. For credit card companies AI is a useful tool for assessing customers' creditworthiness, predicting bankruptcies and detecting fraud.

A variety of AI tools and methods have developed over the decades, one such being "expert systems." Here a computer scientist quizzes an expert on a given subject about all the rules he or she uses in making decisions – for instance how a supermarket manager decides how many boxes of cereals or cartons of milk to put on the shelves. The scientist then builds these rules into software which mimics the expert's decision-making processes along the lines of "if x is true then do y." Creating such a system is laborious work and, to begin with at least, they were not particularly intelligent. However in the 1970s "fuzzy logic" began to be incorporated into expert systems, allowing them to go beyond simply saying whether a proposition was true or false by attaching degrees of likelihood that a statement was true.

Another AI technique is "genetic algorithms." These are computer programs which work in a similar way to how nature allows for survival of the fittest. They imitate natural selection in the way genes are passed from generation to generation to produce offspring best adapted for survival. The programs allow hundreds of thousands of possible solutions to a problem to compete with each other to find the best solution. On financial markets genetic algorithms can be used to search through large amounts of data for so-called predictive signals. This is rooted in the chaos theory and the concept of non-linearity. Chaos theorists believe that all results have a cause but those results are not proportionate to the cause. A seemingly insignificant event can bring about a major consequence. One example comes from folklore:

> **Chaos theorists believe that all results have a cause but those results are not proportionate to the cause.**

> For want of a nail, the shoe was lost,
> For want of a shoe, the horse was lost,
> For want of a horse, the rider was lost,

For want of a rider, a message was lost,
For want of a message, the battle was lost,
For want of a battle, the kingdom was lost.

This is known as the Butterfly Effect: a butterfly beating its wings on one side of the world can set off a chain of events that leads to a hurricane on the other. In the world of finance, chaos theorists reject any notion that markets move in a random fashion and are therefore unpredictable. On the contrary, every market move is triggered by a cause but that original event may seem so insignificant that it is difficult to spot at the time. That's why forecasters need AI methods such as genetic algorithms to sift the tiny event which triggers a disproportionately large market move from all the other events that have no effect. This is the search for the predictive signal.

One of the most common tools of AI is the artificial neural network and it is this "Terminator technology" that Harry Smith is harnessing to predict financial markets better than the human brain, or so he hopes. Smith builds neural networks for Standard Life Investments, a fund manager based at an elegant building in Edinburgh's Georgian New Town.

Getting in the way of a good decision

Artificial neural networks are based on biological neural networks. The brain consists of nerve cells called neurones which allow humans to learn from past experience and sift current information to solve new problems. Artificial neural networks use computer software to mimic these processes of learning and decision making. The trick for financial forecasters is to make these networks not only match the brain's abilities but better them, at least in some respects. "We all have our own biases," says David Jubb, an investment director who leads the AI project at Standard Life. "You have information but possibly the human brain is not making the best out of that information."[2] Jubb, a mathematics graduate of Scotland's St Andrews University, believes that forecasters commonly fail because they interpret financial data to fit their preconceived views of the world. Artificial neural networks, by contrast, harbor no prejudices. "Their interpretation of the data is completely independent. There is no scope for human bias to get in the way of a good decision," says Jubb.

Applying AI to financial markets has not been easy. Much of the early research focused on expert systems because it was thought that neural networks could not work. However, after some breakthroughs investors and scientists began using neural networks to try to predict financial markets in the 1980s. The early days were difficult. In late 1986 economist Halbert White, a professor at the University of California at San Diego, began using a neural network to seek patterns in IBM stock price movements. At an AI conference in 1988 he reported that progress had been slow. "So far only random jumps and dips are evident. It won't be easy to uncover predictable stock market fluctuations with neural networks and if you succeed, you'll probably want to keep it secret," he said. "The present neural network is not a money machine."

Applying AI to financial markets has not been easy.

Undaunted, White and many others have pressed on with their research, which took off as the powerful computers needed to build advanced neural networks became available more cheaply. Today websites offering stock market predictions made by one kind of AI or another are commonplace on the internet. Most are small operations but some heavy hitters of the financial markets are now trying out AI. Standard Life Investments manages over $100 billion in clients' assets and is a subsidiary of Europe's biggest mutually owned life insurance company. The Santa Fe team, whose business is appropriately called Prediction Company, is relatively small but builds trading systems for UBS Warburg, a leading international investment bank whose parent is Switzerland's UBS, one of the 10 biggest banks in the world. Unlike the websites, neither Standard Life nor UBS Warburg sells investments or advice that are driven by AI to the public. For the time being at least they use AI in-house only.

Harry Smith's black box

Harry Smith has no background in finance and works only part time at Standard Life. Three days a week he is an accident and emergency manager at a hospital in the Scottish borders. Financial markets are usually synonymous with high stress levels but Smith ironically finds his two days a week at Standard Life a relief from the strain of working in Britain's overstretched and underfunded National Health Service. His first stab at building a neural network was for the health service, using information on a patient's heartbeat from an electrocardiogram (ECG). "An ECG determines whether a patient is having a heart attack. Could a neural network determine whether there were some hidden features in the ECG which could tell us which patients were going to live or die?" he says. It turned out that this particular system could not, but its failure underlines a basic lesson of neural networks: they are only as good as the data they are given to analyze. "Our tools at that time for looking at heart arrhythmias were not particularly good. We were putting crap in and getting crap out," he says.[3] But Smith adapted the idea when he studied for a Master of Business Administration degree at Edinburgh's Napier University. "There are a lot of similarities between forecasting heart arrhythmias and financial markets," he says. So he toured financial institutions to research his dissertation in 1997 and it was then that he met Jubb at Standard Life. "David asked me if I had any software and could I develop it into some kind of forecasting mechanism," he says. The partnership was therefore born and secrecy began to descend on to the project. Smith refused to give his academic mentor details of the neural network and Napier rejected the dissertation. "The next year I completely ignored neural networks and did a bog standard dissertation. It was absolute garbage," he says. But he got the MBA.

Smith explains how a neural network works using the example of a sports stadium manager who has to order hamburgers and ice creams for each fixture. If he orders too few he loses money by failing to meet the fans' demand. If he orders too many he loses money by wasting food. Demand varies from match to match and it is the neural network's job to reason why: it uses patterns of demand at past matches to forecast sales at future matches. One consideration is naturally how many people watch the games. Factors affecting attendance are legion: more fans come if the home team is playing well in the championship, fewer if it is struggling – unless, of course a top team visits when more locals turn out to watch the star opponents in action. A derby match against a local team may also draw a larger crowd. Next the weather forecast is important. If it's hot the spectators will want more ice creams and fewer hamburgers, while in mid winter demand for the ice creams will be low – unless lots of children attend and nag their parents for an ice despite the chill. So the permutations multiply to the point that our confused stadium manager may fail to see the wood for the trees.

This is where the computer can help by sifting the permutations and making a logical forecast. The manager feeds these individual factors into the neural network, along with examples of how they affected demand at past matches, giving each one a numerical value. They are factors that any forecaster should consider and in a sense the neural network uses classical forecasting techniques. The trick is to process large amounts of information more efficiently. "The whole function of a neural network is to minimize error," says Smith, "The more patterns you give it the better it gets." The network consists of a series of input nodes into which are fed the raw figures as numerical values, and output nodes from which the forecasts emerge. In between lies a series of hidden nodes, all of which are connected to each of the input and output nodes, giving a complex network. Every bit of information or numerical value is multiplied by every other bit. This allows the network to search for complex patterns of demand. These patterns change over time; for instance the home side will move up and down the league table, so the manager must keep giving the network new figures from recent matches so that it can learn new patterns of demand and change its forecasts accordingly.

In financial markets the principles are the same, even though the input and output data are different. Harry Smith's black box will predict stock indices, bonds, currency exchange rates or commodities. Typically, to forecast a stock index you might feed the neural network past rises and falls of the index, details of companies' profitability and productivity, analysts' recommendations of which stocks to buy, hold and sell, and the background such as overall economic growth, inflation and so on. However, Smith and Jubb clam up when asked what data they give their computer. According to the "crap in, crap out" principle, a neural network is only as good as the information it is fed, and they don't want their competitors to know which figures they are using. However, Smith says it is pointless to throw any old data at the computer. "You want the minimum amount of inputs which you know will work," he says.

"We will never get an accurate forecast"

Do neural networks work? At Standard Life the answer was definitely not in the early stages. For the first two years Smith and Jubb back tested the neural network by feeding it old data to see whether it predicted market moves which had subsequently happened. This was not a happy time. "Within a year we identified the major problems with the neural networks," says Smith. "I sat there in front of the computer screen, I recognized the problem and I said we will never get an accurate forecast. There was no way round it. I was close to resigning." But they plugged away using trial and error and the break came in the summer of 1998 when stock markets crashed. "From roughly April onwards we could see the July peak in the markets. As we got closer in time, April, May, June, the peak was still in July," says Jubb.

Economists have blamed a chain of events for the crash, including economic crisis in east Asia, a Russian decision to devalue the rouble and default on part of its debt, and the resulting global panic which brought down the LTCM hedge fund. But Jubb believes that markets would have tumbled anyway. "All the real world things can explain that, but there really was something in the data that we were using, whether it was the price history or some of the indicators we were putting in, that said this market was due a turn and that turn was due in July," he says. "It didn't matter which market, which indicator, which method of forecasting we used, it still came up with that. It was a very powerful message and one we were able to present in advance and say this is serious." On June 11, 1998 Jubb presented a one-page briefing note titled "July 1998 correction – what are we going to do about it?" to Standard Life's Global Investment Group, a committee of fund managers that decides where to invest. "It seems a little bold and provocative now but at the time we were very confident," says Jubb, and rightly so. On July 16, 1998 the Dow Jones Industrial Average peaked at 9328, a month before the Russian devaluation, and by the start of September it had tumbled almost 17 percent. The broader Standard & Poor's 500 index peaked four days later and lost even more. By the end of August it had lost 19 percent. Harry Smith's black box had been right.

A major lesson to be learnt

But the success did not last. In the crisis of the summer and autumn of 1998 panicking investors ditched shares and bought low-risk US Treasury bonds, a traditional safe haven in turbulent times. "There was a big change in the bond market and we got that accurately," says Smith. "Then all of a sudden the neural networks started getting it all wrong. There was a major lesson there to be learnt." In 1999 investors gradually regained their confidence and sold off their holdings of US bonds in search of better returns back in stocks. At this time man proved to be better than machine. "Through 1999 I was bearish on the bond market because of the data I could see but the neural networks never picked it up the whole year," says Jubb. "That was something we worked on very hard in 2000. That is how some of our newer forecasting techniques evolved. You learn from your mistakes and we're always making them."

Jubb refuses to say what information he feeds the neural network but it is much more than the data on past market prices and volume of transactions on which technical analysts base their forecasts. "You can use price history for neural networks and you will get out a forecast. But you've got to provide the neural network with high quality information and in my view price history is not that high quality. A lot of the technical analysts whose work I see will have a view and they will interpret the chart in a bearish or bullish fashion according to what their prior view was."

The strength of the neural network, says Jubb, is that it can handle different patterns in financial markets. For example, an interest rate cut by the US Federal Reserve of a quarter percentage point may boost the stock market one day, and yet the same sized cut may depress prices another day. On one occasion the rate cut might have pleasantly surprised investors; on another it might have disappointed them because they had expected a bigger drop.

The strength of the neural network is that it can handle different patterns in financial markets.

A conventional computer system would assume that a quarter percentage point rate cut would have the same effect on stock prices whatever the circumstances, unless a human being changed the calculations in its program. By contrast a neural network should spot such changes itself, provided it is fed new data showing that the world is a different place. "We rerun the whole forecast every day for each market," says Jubb. "It's not that it takes yesterday's learning and extrapolates forward, it relearns every market every day and produces a forecast." This ability to learn from experience can be a weakness, as well as a strength of the system, at least in explaining neural networks to skeptics, of which there are plenty in the financial markets. "We don't understand totally what they're doing, especially when they come up with something completely different from our own interpretation of the data. It's very difficult to explain the whole thing to people," says Jubb. "There is a formula underneath all that but it's such a complicated formula, and it changes every time it relearns."

At the moment Standard Life uses the neural network only to corroborate forecasts that humans have made using traditional techniques. It is a conservative institution and has to be due to its business. It is no swashbuckling hedge fund managing the investments of wealthy people who should be able to look after themselves. Nor does it trade on its own account. A large chunk of the $100 billion plus it manages is pension fund money on which many people rely for a secure retirement. Other clients are small investors who channel some of their life savings into the stock market via mutual funds. This is not money they can gamble like the rich, it is wealth they can ill-afford to lose.

Jubb works in Standard Life's strategy department advising the seven-strong Global Investment Group on which markets are likely to rise and which are likely to fall, and which sectors will outperform and which will underperform, whether they be high technology stocks, pharmaceuticals makers, media companies or whatever.

The Global Investment Group decides on "asset allocation" – the balance of investments in stocks, bonds, currencies, commodities or cash and in which countries. For example, an asset allocation group may decide to cut its investments in continental European stocks and raise them in US treasury bonds. All these decisions are still made by people, not computers. "We haven't yet got to the stage where we're willing to put money behind the neural network and let it trade to its heart's content," says Jubb. To test the network Jubb and Smith fed in 10 years' data from the Standard & Poor's 500 index and asked it to produce thousands of forecasts for the period. If you flip a coin to decide whether to buy or sell in the long term, you would be right 50 percent of the time. The neural network did better than that, making the right call more than 60 percent of the time. But other forecasting techniques also achieve success rates of over 50 percent. "Are the neural networks picking up better quality information out of the data than we are picking up?" asks Jubb. "We can't say for sure at this stage but it does look like it adds some value." However, on some occasions the humans have been right and the neural network wrong, he admits.

If you flip a coin to decide whether to buy or sell in the long term, you would be right 50 percent of the time.

The biggest challenge for any forecaster is to predict turning points in markets. That's especially tough when speculative bubbles inflate as in the late 1990s. At a time when fear and greed alone dictate prices, traditional forecasting techniques have little to say. "A pyramid will collapse but the big question is when. You can lose an awful lot of money going against it too early. We're looking for the neural network to help in identifying the turning points by looking at the interaction between the price and the various indicators we use," says Jubb. "We use it pretty much for any market where investor psychology plays a large part." Harry Smith's neural network tries to learn human behavior, without succumbing to its weaknesses.

Andrew Milligan, a member of the Global Investment Group, is cautious about using the neural network for anything more than corroboration. "Unexpected events will always happen and they will always be serious," he says. "A lot of these modelling techniques have come a cropper because of this issue. They work for a period of time and then collapse."[4] Twelve days after Milligan made that comment the suicide hijackers attacked America. In the first week of trading after the disaster the Dow tumbled more than 14 percent and the S&P 500 almost 8 percent. How did Standard Life's neural network handle the shock? "Initially it didn't even want to learn the new price structure but it picked it up in subsequent weeks," says Jubb. "A lot of what we're doing is still very much research, not live trading. It's food for thought for us about what you would do in that situation."

Science geeks

For Norman Packard, President of Prediction Company in Santa Fe, the disaster of September 11 and what followed on the stock market was more than mere food for thought. His black boxes don't just predict, they also trade shares actively. Prediction Company produces trading systems for an in-house investment fund at UBS Warburg which are powered partly, but not entirely, by AI. On September 11 that fund was in the thick of the markets with millions of shares on its books. The fund uses AI very differently from Standard Life, but the systems have a common feature: they take time to learn. "When you have a disaster like that, all of a sudden people are thinking about investments in different kinds of ways," says Packard, a former professor of physics at the University of Illinois. "Prices start moving in response to information that is generated by the disaster and it takes a while for that information to enter the price stream and get incorporated into our models."[5] That means for a while the system worked on stale information. A natural inclination might be to shut down the black box and pull out of the market until things return to something like normal. This, however, was not an option. "Our portfolio is so huge it would have cost an enormous amount of money to trade out of all our positions. So we just had to hold on for the ride," says Packard. "We took a big hit in the two trading days succeeding the disaster but within a week after that we had made it all back."

Prediction Company was founded in 1991 by Packard, related distantly to the co-founder of Hewlett-Packard computer company, and fellow physicist Doyne Farmer. Now a professor at the Santa Fe Institute, Farmer once worked at the nearby Los Alamos National Laboratory. During World War Two, Los Alamos was home of the top-secret Manhattan project which built and detonated the first atomic bomb. Nowadays it is the main research and development center for the US nuclear weapons program, although computer science is also part of its work and Farmer set up its Complex Systems Group. A book has been written about the partnership which makes much of how Packard and Farmer, whose preferred dress code was T-shirts and shorts, headed into the dark-suited world of American finance in the early 1990s to sell their ideas. Today Packard tolerates the "science geek" tag but insists that the science is deadly serious. A Chicago brokerage, O'Connor and Associates, spotted the potential of that science in 1992 and agreed to fund development of Prediction Company's trading technology. Through a series of takeovers O'Connor became part of UBS Warburg, which now owns 33 percent of Prediction Company.

Trust the models

Despite Packard's use of "we" when talking about the fund, Prediction Company does no trading. It designs and builds the computer models which are installed on the trading floor at UBS Warburg in Chicago and have traded stocks since 1996. Those models draw on a variety of forecasting techniques. "We're not wedded to any particular one," he says. "We have used neutral networks quite extensively but we have also used other machine learning techniques like genetic algorithms." Packard estimates that AI in the broadest sense produces 40 to 50 percent of its research.

At Standard Life the neural network predicts how markets in general will perform in the coming months, for example, forecasting a stock index rather than an individual stock. In the end a human being still decides which shares, bonds or commodity contracts to buy or sell. By contrast Prediction Company systems not only decide which individual stocks to buy and sell, but also execute the orders. Human intervention is rare. "We just trust the models and we don't trust our ability to have enough information to override the models," says Packard. Here lies a crucial issue: how much faith to place in the black box and how much to overrule it. In this case humans monitor the computers, but in normal operations override them only a handful of times a year out of tens or even hundreds of thousands of trades. One reason for overriding is financial market regulations. If UBS Warburg is doing a deal involving a particular company it may be prohibited from trading the firm's stock. So if the computer wants to buy or sell a prohibited stock a human has to stop it. Another case shows how AI may sift vast amounts of data better than the human brain, but can still fall down on logic. Packard cites a computer software company whose main product is airline reservation systems. Following the attack on America, airline ticket sales collapsed so stocks in companies linked to civil aviation fell far more than the average for the market. "After the disaster it started behaving like an airline stock instead of a software stock but our models were treating it like a software stock. So that was something where we made an override," says Packard. In other words the computer model did not realize what was happening. But Packard says that overriding is rare. "We only did that for 10 or 12 stocks out of a portfolio of between one and two thousand stocks. The amount of overriding that we ended up doing even in these exceptional circumstances right after the disaster was quite small."

Packard has strong although not blind faith in the model's abilities. "This faith comes not from doubting that humans have relevant information but rather from doubting that we have a clean and effective way to combine that human information with the model's information," he says. The trading systems have two layers. One decides what position to take in the market and when it decides that the best position has changed it sends out signals to buy certain stocks and sell others. The second layer executes the orders, meaning the system is automated to keep costs down. Research and development costs notwithstanding a black box is cheaper to run than a highly paid trader, doesn't get sick (give or take the odd crash) and doesn't demand vacations. The UBS Warburg fund is hedged, taking a number of bets that certain stocks will rise equal to bets that other stocks will fall. The models buy shares they expect to rise, taking a long position, and sell short stocks they predict will fall. Having a balanced portfolio of short and long positions reduces risk. If the whole market tumbles the fund will lose money on the stocks it holds but make money on the stocks it has sold short. In a falling market stocks of fundamentally strong companies should drop less than those of firms which are fundamentally weak. So if the hedge fund has chosen well it should make more money on the short positions than it loses on its long positions. This is one way a balanced hedge fund makes its profits.

A black box is cheaper to run than a highly paid trader, doesn't get sick (give or take the odd crash) and doesn't demand vacations.

At UBS Warburg the computer models do more than merely decide which stocks are likely to rise and which are likely to fall. They also construct strategies for hedging and limiting risk involved in the investments. Packard says this is another argument against overriding the models too freely. "We have to be very careful that we're not just … countering something that the model is doing for some complicated set of reasons, having to do not only with predictability but also hedging and risk."

There are times when share analysts recommend buying a stock just as the computer wants to sell it. Packard says the simple answer is to look at past occasions when this happened and check who turned out to be right, man or the machine. As with Standard Life, Packard says it is difficult to discover how the model reaches a decision because so many factors beyond pure prediction are involved. Again hedging, risk control and how actively a given stock is traded come into play. "We have crafted the components to work together so that we can trust them as a whole. Hence we're not incredibly motivated to tease them apart too much," says Packard. "If things do go bad we have banks of tests to try and isolate what's going wrong … That's the closest we get to a detailed explanation of what's going on."

While Jubb is selective in the data he feeds to Standard Life's neural network, Prediction Company has a catholic attitude. "We have practically all the data related to equities that we can lay our hands on. Part of our research is ploughing through all this data and figuring out the different ways to use it," says Packard. That means not just detailed figures on the price of stocks and how much of it trades, but also analysts' forecasts of company earnings, their stock recommendations, information on companies' accounts and so on. "We're not doctrinaire," he says. That means taking neither a purely fundamental approach, like Warren Buffett who bases his decisions on the fundamental strength or weakness of individual companies in which he invests, nor the chart approach of the technical analysts. "[We use] rather a combination of all the data where we can find reliable predictability."

So how well does the fund perform? Sadly Dave Zyer, managing director at UBS Warburg in charge of prediction-based trading in Chicago, won't say. As the fund is in-house, its track record and even its size are confidential. Packard is also bound by a confidentiality clause in Prediction Company's contract with UBS

Warburg. But he says: "We're definitely at the top levels of both size and performance. We have to be there for the bank to maintain its interest."

Notes

1 *Introduction to Artificial Intelligence*, Boyd & Fraser, San Francisco, 1978.

2 Interview with author.

3 Interview with author.

4 Interview with author.

5 Interview with author.

12

Black box, black hole

"We were able to build a portfolio that was essentially riskless."

– Myron Scholes, Nobel prize winner and partner in Long-Term Capital Management[1]

Perhaps unfairly, the shadow of Long-Term Capital Management falls over any venture using black box computer programs. LTCM, after all, was the biggest and boldest of all the hedge funds and its near demise in September 1998 seemed to threaten the stability of the entire financial system.

Hedge funds, as their name suggests, hedge their bets by balancing long and short positions.

Hedge funds, as their name suggests, hedge their bets by balancing long and short positions. UBS Warburg follows a similar strategy but invests only its own money. By contrast, hedge funds seek outside investors to put up capital but they're not the kind of ordinary folk who might put some of their savings into a mutual fund or unit trust of the kind run by Standard Life and its competitors. Hedge funds are exclusive clubs open only to banks and other institutions or very wealthy individuals. One hedge fund manager is well known to the wider public: George Soros. In 1992 Hungarian-born Soros placed a $10 billion bet that Britain would fail to keep sterling in the European exchange rate mechanism, which set bands in which the pound traded against fellow European Union currencies. Speculators led by Soros fought a battle royal with the Bank of England on foreign exchange markets and won. Sterling crashed out of the ERM and Soros made $1 billion on the bet.

Typically, hedge funds are private partnerships and as they are not open to the public they are subject to few of the regulations which aim to protect small investors. Rich banks and rich people are, it is assumed, able to assess risk for themselves. The story of Long-Term Capital Management suggests this may not be true.

The Master of the Universe

LTCM was the brainchild of an Irish-American from Chicago called John Meriwether. Meriwether had run an immensely profitable bond trading operation at the Wall Street firm Salomon Brothers, which earned him the nickname "Master of the Universe," but in 1991 he was forced out in the first scandal of his career involving a relatively junior trader. Meriwether refused to go gracefully. He regrouped much of his old team as the LTCM partnership and went into business in 1994 using the strategy which had proved so successful at Salomon Brothers. One of his coups was to recruit David Mullins, the Vice Chairman of the Federal Reserve, suggesting that he had been rehabilitated following the Salomon scandal.

LTCM had a bank of computers at its headquarters in leafy Greenwich, Connecticut, to run its complex investment strategy. But rather than using artificial intelligence, it relied on the intelligence of its team, made up of Meriwether's bond traders and academics recruited from America's top universities including Harvard and the Massachusetts Institute of Technology (MIT). LTCM's brightest academic stars were Robert Merton and Myron Scholes, who won the Nobel prize for economics in 1997 – ironically just as the fund was running into trouble. In a book on the fiasco, *When Genius Failed*,[2] financial writer Roger Lowenstein played down the role of computers in a strategy based largely on expectations that the gap, or "spread," between yields on US Treasury bonds and other more risky bonds would narrow over time.

"The common notion that Long-Term had a unique black box was a myth. Other Wall Street firms had also found their way to MIT, and most of the big banks were employing similar models – and, what's more, were applying them to the same couple of dozen spreads in bond markets," he wrote. "Long-Term's edge wasn't in its models but, first, in its experience in *reading* the models. The partners had been doing such trades for years." The second factor in LTCM's edge was the ability of Meriwether and partners to arrange financing from dozens of banks on liberal terms.

Lowenstein describes how LTCM's strategy of "arbitraging" was developed when Meriwether and much of his team were still at Salomon Brothers. "They downloaded into their computers all of the past bond prices they could get their hands on. They distilled the bonds' historical relationships, and they modelled how these prices should behave in the future. And then, when a market price somewhere, somehow, got out of line, the computer model told them."

Meriwether's band of mathematician-traders believed that markets were efficient and would therefore inevitably iron out such "inefficiencies." This would eventually bring the value of assets such as bonds, or options to buy or sell bonds, back towards their "true" value as calculated by the computer models. All LTCM had to do was place bets on this happening, wait for the anomaly to disappear and collect their profits. The computers used calculations developed from a formula which Scholes and the late physicist-mathematician Fischer Black had published in 1973 to calculate the value of a stock option. An option is a kind of financial derivative contract, related to an insurance policy, which allows – but does not oblige – the holder to buy or sell shares at a later date for a pre-agreed price. The holder exercises the option only if he can make money on it. Merton later adapted the formula to allow the value of an option to be continually recalculated and risk supposedly continually eliminated by hedging. It was this work that won Scholes and Merton their Nobel prizes. Black died in 1995 before he could collect a gong.

Betting a billion

At first LTCM shied way from the unpredictable stock markets so the black box got to work mainly on bonds and bond derivatives. For the strategy to make LTCM's partners and clients rich, it had to be conducted on a grand scale. Often the margins of profit were paper thin. If you bet $1 million and the margin is 1 percent, you make only $10,000, a paltry sum for the likes of Meriwether. But if you bet $1 billion the profit is a more satisfactory $10 million. Scholes likened the strategy to using a gigantic vacuum cleaner to suck up nickels from all over the world. Naturally the best laid plans can come to grief, so to bet such huge amounts LTCM used mathematics to eliminate risk – or at least it thought it had. "The broad strategy of LTCM was to figure out how to hedge out the risks of your position such that you can do a lot of it, much more than you can do if you didn't hedge out the risks," said Scholes.[3]

Scholes likened the strategy to using a gigantic vacuum cleaner to suck up nickels from all over the world.

After a slow start, LTCM raised $1.25 billion for its launch in February 1994 from a range of investors, private and institutional, in the United States and beyond. The names included Sumitomo Bank of Japan, Dresdner Bank of Germany and even the Italian central bank. UBS didn't join up immediately but did later, with disastrous results. But $1.25 billion wasn't enough. For the strategy to work, LTCM needed to borrow huge amounts of money to magnify the bets, and consequently the profits when they paid off. Naturally if the bets did not pay off, the losses would likewise be magnified, but the LTCM partners were confident they had the risks all worked out. The clients also seemed happy, although they had little idea of how the fund was investing their money. Even if they had asked, LTCM wouldn't have told them. Secrecy is a watchword in the world of hedge funds and the strategy depended on LTCM placing bets on the anomalies before anybody else had spotted them. Few of the investors can have been inclined to ask questions in the first few years because the results spoke for themselves. Investors enjoyed returns of about 40 percent in 1995 and also in 1996, even after paying LTCM's huge fees.

In 1997 LTCM's return after fees dropped just below 20 percent, still an exceptional performance. Despite its secrecy other investors had cottoned on and started aping its strategy, closing bond market anomalies before LTCM could get to them. LTCM tried moving into stocks but with investment opportunities dwindling, it returned $2.7 billion to its investors at the end of 1997. That reduced its capital by more than a third to $4.8 billion but, startlingly, LTCM did not cut the size of its investments. Its levels of debt, in proportion to its capital, therefore went through the roof.

Already in 1997 financial markets were becoming unsettled and some investors were growing increasingly "risk averse." That means they drifted away from investments which gave a good return but at the price of higher risk, and into those which offered a lower return but greater security. None offered greater security than Treasury bonds, guaranteed by the US government itself. A major source of insecurity at the time was a domino dive in stock markets, currencies and ultimately entire economies in east Asia, which began with Thailand and spread through much of the region. For LTCM this ought not to have been too much of a problem. After all, it was well hedged and its investments were well diversified around the globe both in wealthy western nations and in the developing economies of east Asia, Latin America and post-communist eastern Europe. These are known as "emerging markets" although as one after another succumbed to the contagion traders began to call them "submerging markets."

The bolt from the blue

The end came in 1998. The bolt from the blue struck on August 17, 1998, to be precise, when Russia devalued the rouble and effectively defaulted on its short-term debt. Russia's action triggered a "flight to quality" and in this case quality meant US Treasury bonds. LTCM had tried to limit risk by putting money into a wide range of investments in a wide range of countries. If one market started going the wrong way, others would compensate by going the right way. Rather than bailing out of individual investments or individual countries, however, investors deserted anything or anywhere that seemed risky. It was this contagion that brought LTCM to its knees.

Prices of riskier bonds tumbled while those of US Treasuries soared. Consequently yields, which move in the opposite direction to prices, fell on Treasuries and rose on riskier bonds. So much for the Nobel laureates' assumptions that yield spreads would narrow over time: in the summer of 1998 they were widening rapidly.

A US government report into the fiasco the following year dryly summed up the problem: "Both LTCM and other market participants suffered losses in individual markets that greatly exceeded what conventional risk models, estimated during more stable periods, suggested were probable. Moreover, the simultaneous shocks to many markets confounded expectations of relatively low correlations between market prices and revealed that global trading portfolios like LTCM's were less well diversified than assumed."[4] Scholes put it more simply: "After the Russian default ... all the relations that tended to exist in the recent past seemed to disappear."

The report, signed among others by Fed Chairman Alan Greenspan and Treasury Secretary Robert Rubin, gave a glimpse of the web of LTCM investments. These included bonds issued by governments and corporations in both the developed and emerging economies, plus stocks and derivatives. LTCM took positions on about a dozen futures exchanges worldwide, mainly in interest rate and stock index futures contracts. These allow investors to bet on future changes in interest rates and in the leading stock market indices, respectively. Outside organized markets LTCM took out "over-the-counter" (OTC) derivatives contracts with several dozen institutions, including swap, forward and options contracts focused on interest rate and equity markets. The report revealed the staggering sums involved. "The Fund reportedly had over 60,000 trades on its books, including long securities positions of over $50 billion and short positions of an equivalent magnitude. At the end of August, 1998, the gross notional amounts of the Fund's contracts on futures exchanges exceeded $500 billion, swaps contracts more than $750 billion, and options and other OTC derivatives over $150 billion," it said.

There was nothing notional about LTCM's losses as the markets turned against it.

In August 1998 alone LTCM lost $1.8 billion and its capital was running out fast. By the end of the month it had only $2.3 billion left of the $4.8 billion that it began the year with, and still it was losing heavily. Meriwether and his partners desperately searched for new capital, sounding out Buffett and Soros among others, but nothing came of it. As word got round of LTCM's problems the generous lending on liberal terms that its bankers had supplied in the good years began to dry up. For a fund as heavily indebted as LTCM the situation became critical. By September fears grew that

LTCM would default, dragging down the companies with which it was trading – which included some of the biggest names on Wall Street – and threatening a wider collapse in the financial system.

Meltdown

Faced with a possible market meltdown the Federal Reserve Bank of New York, the Fed's eyes and ears on Wall Street, stepped in. Its president, William McDonough, "invited" LTCM's major creditors to the New York Fed to sort out the mess. In the resulting bailout 14 banks and brokerages put up $3.6 billion, led by the big institutions such as Merrill Lynch, Goldman Sachs and UBS which put up $300 million each. In return the consortium won operational control of LTCM and a 90 percent stake in it. Meriwether and his partners saw their stake shrivel to just 10 percent. For UBS, the biggest investor in LTCM, the losses did not stop there. It announced it would take a loss of 940 million Swiss francs (around $700 million) on its dalliance with the fund. The Chairman of UBS, Mathis Cabiallavetta, stepped down following the disclosure. For just about everyone involved John Meriwether's black box fund had proved to be little more than a black hole.

For just about everyone involved John Meriwether's black box fund had proved to be little more than a black hole.

The Federal Reserve is supposed to protect the interests of the American economy rather than the interests of very wealthy banks and individuals on Wall Street. But Greenspan subsequently defended the rescue, in which no public money was involved. "Had the failure of LTCM triggered the seizing up of markets substantial damage could have been inflicted on many market participants, including some not directly involved with the firm, and could have potentially impaired the economies of many nations, including our own," he said.[5]

Following the rescue Meriwether was not the most popular man around town but for some people the LTCM debacle discredited the very concept of black box funds. In a statement issued shortly after the bailout Meriwether seemed to suggest that the fund would raise new money and carry on. "Has this guy got any shame?" the *Financial Times* quoted an unnamed banker as saying. "He brings us to the brink with his black box nonsense and then has the balls to say we did it to keep him in work."[6]

Lessons of the fiasco

LTCM's computer programs used relatively conventional mathematical formulae, however complex, rather than artificial intelligence. LTCM also employed a team of traders who made the investment decisions, rather than allowing the black box to trade away undisturbed. Nevertheless Packard admits the LTCM affair, in which UBS was so badly stung, had worried him at first. "I expected to run into a fair amount of internal skepticism because they were such big players in that fiasco. In point of fact everybody kept a very cool and reasonable head throughout that time," he says. "They were looking at our portfolio and what our models were doing, and we got not a hint of any concern of that nature." At UBS Warburg Zyer dismisses any comparison with his fund. "This is totally different from LTCM," he says baldly.

Naturally Packard and Jubb are keen to emphasize the differences between their ventures and LTCM. LTCM's biggest bets were on bonds and derivatives where regulations designed to limit risk are laxer or non-existent. Many of its deals were struck outside any organized market. By contrast the UBS Warburg fund trades on equity markets where regulations set limits on short selling of stocks and borrowing money to fund speculation. "We aren't using that much leverage," says Packard. "Our models are much more automated in the sense that even though they [LTCM] were using formulas to guide the bets they were placing on the interest rates, there were definitely traders there … making decisions in between their formulas and the markets."

The strategies of an unregulated hedge fund are a world apart from conservative Edinburgh fund management, where risk controls are tight. "[LTCM] didn't adopt a sensible risk approach," says Jubb. "They would make a bad trade then they would double it. If it went wrong they would double it again," he says. "Much as we like to promote an aggressive, active management policy, we're not in the business of seeing funds going bust."

Notes

1 Speaking on *The Midas Touch*, BBC TV Horizon program, December 2, 1999.

2 *When Genius Failed*, by Roger Lowenstein, Random House, 2000.

3 Speaking on *The Midas Touch*, BBC TV Horizon program, December 2, 1999.

4 Report of the President's Working Group on Financial Markets on Hedge Funds, Leverage, and the Lessons of Long-Term Capital Management, published April 29, 1999, available at www.treas.gov/press/releases/docs/hedgfund.pdf

5 Testifying before the Banking Committee of the US House of Representatives, October 1, 1998.

6 Quoted in the *Financial Times*, September 25, 1998.

13

Seer suckers?

"No matter how much evidence exists that seers do not exist, suckers will pay for the existence of seers."

– J. Scott Armstrong's "Seer-Sucker Theory"

Peter Bernstein tells a story about Kenneth Arrow, a professor at Stanford University who won the Nobel prize for economics in 1972. During World War Two, Arrow was a meteorologist with the US air force. In the 1940s science could predict the weather for the next couple of days at most but an air force general ordered Arrow and his group to produce forecasts for a month ahead. After a while Arrow checked back on his forecasts and found they were no better than random predictions pulled out of a hat. So he sent a message up the chain of command admitting that his work had no value whatsoever and asking to be relieved of the duty. Back came the answer: "The Commanding General is well aware that the forecasts are no good. However, he needs them for planning purposes."[1] Bernstein, who also served in the US air force prior to a 50-year career on Wall Street, tells this anecdote with a sigh. "This is what feeds the appetite for hard number forecasting," he says. "Even though many people know they're unreliable it's good to have a number. The market for it is insatiable."

Bernstein is the only person in this book who admits to realizing he could not forecast. Period. But does the work of the Market Prophets, like Arrow's weather forecasts, have no value whatsoever? Summing up the case for the prosecution, the evidence is strong that economic and market forecasts, if not worthless, are certainly of limited value. Trying to predict the markets, be it stock prices or currency exchange rates, is particularly hit and miss. To quote Charlie Bean at the Bank of England: "That really is a mug's game."[2] With the exception of a few lone wolves most gurus missed the two biggest stories of the 1990s, the quadrupling of the US market and the 75 percent collapse of the Japanese market. How many stock analysts, highly paid and renowned though they may be, warned you that Enron would collapse? Certainly not the 12 out of 17 "experts" who recommended holding on to or even buying its stock early in December 2001, the month that it filed for bankruptcy protection in the biggest corporate failure in American history. How little they knew. The record on the $1.2 trillion-a-day currency markets is just as bad. Again most forecasters missed the biggest story of the late 1990s, if not the decade: the slide which wiped almost a third off the euro's value. Worse still, Lehman Brothers proved that flipping a coin tells you more about which way currencies will move than serious economic analysis.

> Summing up the case for the prosecution, the evidence is strong that economic and market forecasts, if not worthless, are certainly of limited value.

Perhaps those who predict economies have a better record. With a little detective work Market Prophets can predict next month's inflation rate quite well. But give them a more volatile indicator, such as the whims of the consumer as reflected in retail sales data, and they struggle. Often Fed watchers tell you quite accurately whether Alan Greenspan will change interest rates soon, but mainly because he drops hints for his own selfish reasons. When economists look much further than the next few months they falter. Before he realized he couldn't forecast, Peter Bernstein won a $5000 prize for a prediction of inflation that was out by almost a third, but still better than anyone else managed. Economists repeatedly fail to spot recessions, often even after they've begun. Worse still, so do the policymakers whom we trust to steer our economies on a steady course. In America, Greenspan hesitated too long in 1990 with the result that unemployment kept rising longer than it should have; in 2001 he moved faster but not soon enough to avert a recession, insofar as even maestros can avert them at all. In Britain bad forecasts contributed to Nigel Lawson's blunders that tipped the nation into a boom and bust. When political careers are at risk exasperation grows of the kind that made Ken Clarke consider firing his own forecasting team. Market Prophets can increase their chances by predicting in ranges but that sacrifices precision and doesn't guarantee success. Anyway percentage probabilities and fan charts that encompass all likelihoods provoke derision in dealing rooms, where Harry Truman's two-handed economists are rarely welcome.

In the world of Market Prophecy does reputation count? It means a lot in terms of airtime and column inches devoted to the most renowned forecasters, but it means less in terms of accuracy. The IMF, no doubt for very good reasons, doesn't predict as well as other economists; the Wall Street giants often underperform banks and brokerages that struggle to gain much public recognition. Some individuals outperform the pack that

In the world of Market Prophecy does reputation count?

huddles around the consensus forecast. But no one can predict consistently better; it's rarely the same lone wolves which pop up top over time in the rankings of forecast accuracy. It's no easier to spot the best forecaster until after the event than it is to spot the fastest rising share or the quickest growing economy – the oldest dilemma for the investor. In that respect Market Prophets differ frustratingly little from the markets and economies that they predict.

Market Prophets are particularly poor at foretelling bad events, the recession or the stock market slump, which is when we most need them. Of course there are a few professional pessimists but only by permanently predicting doom, which can cost us a lot of money in the good times, can they ever be right. As in comedy, says Peter Osler, it's all about timing, and Market Prophets have little to say to Groucho Marx or Tony Hancock about that. Perhaps analysts should forget about trying to establish the fundamental value of stocks, or currencies or hogs' bellies, and retreat to the charts and the psychology of the market. But were technical analysts any better at telling us the US stock market was a bubble and when it would burst? The answer is no. Should Market Prophets hand over the job of forecasting to computers? If it were safe to entrust our investments to AI programs everyone would already be doing so. Standard Life Investments use AI only to corroborate forecasts produced by humans. Maybe one day computers will do the job, but not yet.

Maybe one day computers will do the job, but not yet.

Things are getting better?

Is there hope for the future? Given the huge effort that has gone into improving the science, is forecasting getting better? Roy Batchelor thinks so, but not much. "We know macro economic forecasts are getting better in a sense of point accuracy. The average error is coming down over time. On the whole we've weeded out some bad methods; we're doing the best we can with the data. There's been a pay off in tiny improvements in predictive accuracy," he says.[3] Even much maligned equity analysts are raising their game. "What you see is not always very edifying in the sense that the forecasts don't look fantastic," he says. "But whatever investment analysts are doing it's slightly better than the crude forecasting methods that might have been used 10 or 20 years ago."

No one speaks with more authority on the subject than Victor Zarnowitz, who published his first evaluation of the accuracy of economic forecasts (he calls it a "small book") in 1967. He is less certain. "If we learn from evaluation presumably we can somewhat improve the forecasts but it's difficult with turning points, particularly with upper turning points," he says. It shouldn't be so because there are new tools, leading indicators which warn of events ahead. "Some kind of a bias persists. It's very unpopular to predict a peak,

More than 2000 years after Aeschylus, Cassandras remain unloved and often ignored.

of course." More than 2000 years after Aeschylus, Cassandras remain unloved and often ignored.

At Standard Life Investments, Andrew Milligan is yet more pessimistic. "Forecasting techniques are statistically superior but it's a more volatile environment than in the past," he says. "I'm sure it's more difficult now in the sense that we have a more complex environment, not just financial markets but a more complex society and economy." In the past decade a string of surprises has rocked the global economy such as recession in the United States, crises in Asia and Russia, and the technology boom and bust. "All of these have been major events in financial markets which were very difficult to analyze at the time, let alone to forecast," says Milligan. Timing remains the big problem. "The IMF and World Bank are very good at producing tables showing the pressures building up on developing countries but they are the first to admit that they can't give any indication of the timing. It's the volcano principle. What is the likelihood that Mount Etna will have a major explosion in the next 20 years? The likelihood is 90 percent. What's the likelihood it will happen tomorrow? Answer: one percent. The day after? One percent. We know that at some point over the next 10 to 20 years Etna will blow, but each day the risk is very low."

More time with the family?

Should we blame the Market Prophets and policymakers for their shortcomings? In the end they have little to work on beyond data which in the case of the economy is usually late, frequently revised and sometimes simply wrong. Here we are, still arguing whether the New Economy has existed in the United States for the past five years or more. The statistics are simply not clear, or reliable enough to settle the dispute. We should spare a thought for Charlie Bean and his colleagues as they steer monetary policy in a fog, peering into the rear-view mirror for clues to the road ahead. In the case of Enron the data was not only wrong but deliberately so. Who could possibly expect Market Prophets to foresee the turbulent market and economic events that followed September 11, 2001? The CIA and FBI failed to spot such a murderous attack being carefully planned for months or years under their very noses. Who could expect stock analysts to predict the fall of Enron when much of the evidence was hidden from view?

Perhaps no one. But the fact remains that Market Prophets offer us forecasts on the economy and the markets, day in day out, in the full knowledge that they are likely to be wrong – even without the Exogenous Shocks that are simply unpredictable in the strictest sense of the word. Therefore should they not all haul up the white flag and, like Peter Bernstein, admit that they cannot forecast? Should they not flip a coin, or enter today's rate as tomorrow's forecast, shut down the computer and spend more time with their families?

Seat of your pants

In Edinburgh, a city of many noted advocates, Milligan leads the case for the defense. "Is tomorrow going to be like today? If you say yes, then of course you don't carry out any research but you also don't make many decisions," he says. "If you don't think tomorrow is going to be like today then you need to make a forecast. How is it going to be different and where is it going to be different? Most forecasters do not have very sophisticated models. It comes down to their judgment and experience."

Even Ken Clarke, that ever cheerful skeptic, accepts that if you have to make a decision you need a forecast, however awful it might be. "You obviously cannot construct macro economic policy simply relying on the seat of your pants and anecdotal evidence of people you talk to. It has to be done on a rational basis and that involves having serious academic economic forecasts. My skepticism is that you mustn't worship them. You must realize that the forecasts, whoever produces them, are likely to be wrong and all you're getting is the best estimate, sometimes guesstimate, that a team of reasonably intelligent people can produce," he says.

This assumes that you're better off with a forecast than without one. The Lehman Brothers study and the Enron experience suggest that sometimes you're not. It's especially alarming if forecasts are deliberately misleading, if someone who poses as an independent stock analyst is no more than a salesman in disguise. But let's not damn the entire industry for the failings, malicious or unintentional, of some. Often Market Prophets do a good job: especially in the short term they predict interest rates, inflation rates and even GDP quite well. Even when they're wrong they serve a purpose. Expectations play a significant role in markets and economies, and forecasters reveal what people expect. Without a consensus forecast no one would know whether the latest inflation rate or GDP figure was

> But let's not damn the entire industry for the failings, malicious or unintentional, of some. Often Market Prophets do a good job.

higher, lower or in line with expectations. In the great game that is financial markets Market Prophets allow people to make money precisely by getting things wrong sometimes. No one ever made money in a market where nothing was ever a surprise. As Danny Gabay said: "On a month to month basis your probability of hitting the number spot on is very low. Numbers can be quite widely wrong. You're always prone to those shocks but that's what gets the market moving."[4] At the City University, Roy Batchelor agrees that getting the forecast right is not always paramount. "What matters is profitability rather than accuracy ... You can be wildly wrong for a lot of the time and the errors don't matter in financial terms as long as you're right when the big move happens," he says.[5]

The Seer-Sucker theory

A couple of decades ago J. Scott Armstrong, a professor of marketing at the University of Pennsylvania, laid out the Seer-Sucker theory.[6] Armstrong argued that people were willing to pay heavily for expert advice despite evidence that the money was poorly spent. He disputed the suggestion that experience counts, citing a study which tested the ability of three groups. One held doctorates in psychology and the second comprised trainees in psychology. The third were "naive subjects," inexperienced undergraduates. Each group listened to interviews with three clients and predicted how each of them would fill out three personality tests. As one would expect the naïve subjects performed worst, but there was no difference in accuracy between the PhDs and the trainees. "Some expertise seems to lead to a higher level of accuracy in forecasting change; beyond a minimal level, however, additional expertise does not improve accuracy – and there is even some evidence that it may decrease accuracy," he wrote. Assuming this evidence also holds true for financial forecasts, how come people still seek expert advice? "One explanation is that the client is not interested in accuracy, but only in avoiding responsibility. A client who calls in the best wizard available avoids blame if the forecasts are inaccurate. The evasion of responsibility is one possible explanation for why stock market investors continue to purchase expert advice in spite of overwhelming evidence that such advice is worthless," he said.

A client who calls in the best wizard available avoids blame if the forecasts are inaccurate.

Armstrong offered some advice. "Since all available evidence suggests that expertise beyond an easily achieved minimum is of little value in forecasting change, the most obvious advice is to hire inexpensive experts," he wrote. Mary Meeker adieu. "Also, look for unbiased experts – those who are not actually involved in the situation." If we believe Arthur Levitt, that rules out a good chunk of the equity analysis profession. "Finally, there is safety in numbers," Armstrong suggested. Forget about the wunderkind and stick to the consensus. Finally he lays down a challenge. "The conditions under which the seer-sucker theory holds are not well known – it may or may not apply to all areas of forecasting. However, in view of the evidence, it seems wise to put the burden of proof upon the experts to show that their expertise in a given area is valuable."

This advice and challenge predicted much of the debate when the dot.com bubble burst. Two decades after the Seer-Sucker theory appeared Byron Wien, Morgan Stanley's Wall Street veteran, offered a defense of analysts. "In spite of all the criticism of Wall

Street research, it is clear that analysts have an influence on the market for their stocks. When an analyst changes a recommendation a stock often moves abruptly in one direction or another even if the analyst isn't an all-star," he wrote. "Portfolio managers have only limited fundamental knowledge of the stocks they follow and often respond quickly to the views of others they have reason to respect. After all they have to keep up with what's happening in the world, the economy and a variety of industries. Many of them own more than a hundred stocks and have some knowledge of a hundred more. It goes back to priorities. How much knowledge can you huddle in your brain? The result is that you rely on others inside and outside your own firm. When an apparently knowledgeable outsider gets more positive or negative, many feel compelled to take action, if only defensively."[7]

Wien is right. Analysts' recommendations do influence stock prices. But he wrote this more than a year before Enron collapsed. These days the argument that fund managers can rely on the views of others they have reason to respect – that means analysts – seems a little weak.

Modesty is sometimes in short supply on the markets, notably in equity analysis.

Modesty is sometimes in short supply on the markets, notably in equity analysis. But it's striking how many economists in particular admit to the weakness of their work. Zarnowitz laments that forecasters work in a market which needs point forecasts. "That's a wrong demand in a sense because you cannot satisfy it with the present state of the art or knowledge. Perhaps it will never be possible to be accurate in economic forecasting. There are simply too many factors at play. There are millions of them and millions of individual decisions. Economics is built on strong assumptions of rationality and optimising but unfortunately human nature is different," he says. "All forecasts should be recognized as probabilistic."[8] Anyone making forecasts and anyone using them has to accept that some things simply cannot be predicted. It's a waste of time trying to allow for "exogenous shocks." "What can you do with the shocks? They are always with us. Some are positive, some are negative, some are long lasting, some are short lasting; some are real, some are monetary. The economy doesn't always respond the same way," he says. "Economic policies could not deal with a terrorist attack, for example. You can at best respond after the fact."

Responding after the fact is precisely what every forecaster and policymaker had to do after September 11, 2001. When Charlie Bean was interviewed for this book, he was trying to fathom the economic consequences of the attacks with precious little data to work on. Almost all the available statistics had been collected before September 11. Nevertheless he was working to a clear deadline: little more than a week later he, and the other members of the Monetary Policy Committee, had to decide whether to give the British economy a psychological and monetary boost by cutting interest rates. In the event they did cut the repo rate. But Bean admitted that his profession was not necessarily best placed to reach a conclusion. "What's going to happen over the next few months, or year or two, in the wake of the September 11 events? We obviously have to make a stab at it here at the Bank but political scientists and military strategists may have as much to say as economists – or even psychologists," he said. "There is too much attention paid to forecasts and that's often an area where economists don't have a lot to say."[9]

At the IMF, Loungani agrees that forecasts figure too highly. "People think that's what economists are paid for. But most economists think they are paid for a lot more than just telling you what comes next. They get paid for analysis that can be after the fact analysis," he says. "We didn't call it but now it's happened we can tell you why it happened and what to do to get out of it." This might excuse Greenspan's poor predicting record. "Even if he gets the forecast wrong his job is to give us the right policy advice."

Ken Clarke offers a dose of common sense: use forecasts by all means but use them with care. Don't do a Nigel Lawson. His advice applies as much to anyone taking a bet on the stock market as to a chancellor running the economy. "Nobody has solved the problem of exact forecasting of economic activity. It's one of the fascinations of economic policy making: it is unpredictable ... I used to treat the forecasts as interesting sources of information among many other sources of information. I did not regard them as tablets of stone," he says. "The danger for policymakers comes when they become quite consumed by these forecasts, and allow the forecasts to determine the shape of policy in such an inflexible fashion that the policy goes wrong when the forecast goes wrong."

> Use forecasts by all means but use them with care. Don't do a Nigel Lawson.

Perhaps Charles Goodhart, a professor at the London School of Economics since leaving the MPC, sums up best the paradox of prediction. "Nobody is more aware of how bad their forecasts are than the people who've actually done them," he says. "But even so, what else have you got other than gut feeling?"[10]

Notes

1 Bernstein told this anecdote in an interview with the author but it is also to be found in his book on the history of risk *Against the Gods*, John Wiley & Sons Inc, 1996.

2 Interview with author.

3 Interview with author.

4 Interview with author.

5 Interview with author.

6 The Seer-Sucker Theory: The Value of Experts in Forecasting, Published in *Technology Review*, June/July, 1980, 16–24, available at www-marketing.wharton.upenn.edu/forecast/paperpdf/seersucker.pdf

7 The Value of Security Analysis, by Byron Wien, published in Morgan Stanley Dean Witter's *US Investment Perspectives*, July 19, 2000.

8 Interview with author.

9 Interview with author.

10 Interview with author.

further reading

Suggested reading

The library of forecasting books is vast but much of it is impenetrable without specialist knowledge. The following is a non-comprehensive pot-pourri of books, most of which are aimed at the layman and have entertainment as well as academic value.

Steven B. Achelis, *Technical Analysis for A to Z*, McGraw-Hill, 2001.
All you ever wanted to know about the subject. The book is also available online. See below.

Thomas A. Bass, *The Predictors*. Penguin, 1999.
The story of the Prediction Company.

Peter L. Bernstein, *Against the Gods*, John Wiley & Sons Inc, 1996.
The definitive history of risk with plenty on forecasts good and bad.

Alan Blinder, Charles Goodhart, Philipp Hildebrand, David Lipton and Charles Wyplosz, *How Central Banks Talk*, International Center for Monetary and Banking Studies Geneva and Centre for Economic Policy Research, London, 2001.
All about how central banks try to get their message over.

Christopher Cerf and Victor Navasky, *The Experts Speak*, Villard Books, 1998.
An amusing compendium of lousy forecasts, financial and otherwise.

John Maynard Keynes, *The General Theory of Employment, Interest and Money*, Prometheus Books, reprinted 1997.

A revolutionary work of modern economics when it was published in 1936. It's not for the layman but Chapter 12, The State of Long-Term Expectation, is a famous study of the psychology of the stock market.

Roger Lowenstein, *When Genius Failed*, Fourth Estate, new edition 2002.
The story of Long-Term Capital Management.

Burton G. Malkiel, *A Random Walk Down Wall Street*, WW Norton, revised edition 2000.
Explodes many Wall Street myths.

Paul Ormerod, *The Death of Economics*, Faber and Faber, 1995.
A skeptic lambasts orthodox economics.

William Sherden, *The Fortune Sellers*, John Wiley & Sons Inc, 2000.
A critical look at all kinds of forecasting.

Robert J. Shiller, *Irrational Exuberance*, Princeton University Press, new edition 2001.
How investors behave when they get carried away.

Louise Yamada, *Market Magic*, John Wiley & Sons Inc, 1998.
How a leading technical analyst viewed the world before the high-tech bubble burst. The subtitle is "Riding the Greatest Bull Market of the Century."

Suggested websites

The same rules apply as for the books. Naturally there's much, much more but a decent search engine will quickly unearth plenty of interesting sites. All the following addresses worked when I finished the book. More than that I cannot promise.

www.aaai.org/
Website of the American Association for Artificial Intelligence.

www.bankofengland.co.uk

Includes the Bank's quarterly inflation report and lots of useful background on how a central bank works.

www.boj.or.jp/en

The Bank of Japan.

www.ecb.int

The European Central Bank's website.

www.equis.com/free/taaz/index.html

A detailed A–Z of technical analysis, an online version of the Achelis book listed above.

www.federalreserve.gov

Website of the Federal Reserve Board.

www.forecasting.cwru.edu/FAQs/faqs

Frequently asked questions section of the International Institute of Forecasting's website.

www.imf.org

The International Monetary Fund's World Economic Outlook is available here.

www.marketing.wharton.upenn.edu/forecast

Useful site on principles of forecasting.

www.morganstanley.com

Site includes a sample of research produced by the investment bank.

www.nber.org

All you ever needed to know about US recessions going back to the 19th century.

www.news.bbc.co.uk/hi/english/static/audio_video/programmes/analysis/transcripts/tales.txt

Transcript of an entertaining BBC Radio programme about the difficulties of economic forecasting.

www.treas.gov/press/releases/docs/hedgfund.pdf

A US government report on hedge funds after the LTCM fiasco.

www.wws.princeton.edu/~pkrugman/

The website of Princeton economist and pundit Paul Krugman. His old site at the Massachusetts Institute of Technology web.mit.edu/krugman/www/ still carries interesting material.

index

More power to your [business-mind]

Even at the end there's more we can learn. More that *we* can learn from your experience of this book, and more ways to add to *your* learning experience.

For who to read, what to know and where to go in the world of business, visit us at **business-minds.com**.

Here you can find out more about the people and ideas that can make you and your business more innovative and productive. Each month our e-newsletter, *Business-minds Express,* delivers an infusion of thought leadership, guru interviews, new business practice and reviews of key business resources directly to you. Subscribe for free at

▶ **www.business-minds.com/goto/newsletters**

Here you can also connect with ways of putting these ideas to work. Spreading knowledge is a great way to improve performance and enhance business relationships. If you found this book useful, then so might your colleagues or customers. If you would like to explore corporate purchases or custom editions personalised with your brand or message, then just get in touch at

▶ **www.business-minds.com/corporatesales**

We're also keen to learn from your experience of our business books – so tell us what you think of this book and what's on *your* business mind with an online reader report at business-minds.com. Together with our authors, we'd like to hear more from you and explore new ways to help make these ideas work at

▶ **www.business-minds.com/goto/feedback**

[www.business-minds.com
www.financialminds.com]

Incisive, informative, impartial news and stories from the best of Reuters photographers and journalists

FRONTLINES

Ed. Nicholas Moore

ISBN 1903 68401 3

Think of the major news stories of the post-war era, the places where they unfolded and the personalities involved…

"C19? That's the execution cell. You're lucky, mate, to come out of there alive." – *Sandy Gall, on being held in a Ugandan death cell.*

THE ART OF SEEING

Ed. Ulli Michel

ISBN 0 273 65011 4

"Pictures marking most of the world's great events over the past 15 years, mostly of conflict, but also of great beauty, the work of masters of their art." – The Star, *South Africa*

The Art of Seeing offers a fascinating selection of news pictures taken by Reuters photographers who have had the vision and ability to see and capture extraordinary incidents. This collection comprises a story with many threads: celebration, adversity, conflict, diplomacy, triumph and disaster – and offers some of the most spectacular, disturbing and significant images you will ever see.

BRANDS IN THE BALANCE

Kevin Drawbaugh

ISBN 0 273 65035 1

"An intelligent, informative and highly readable book about any organisation's most important assets – their brands. This book is a great contribution to the history and future possibilities of branding. It is recommended for anyone with an interest in brands, whether brand lovers, or brand sceptics." – *Rita Clifton, CEO, Interbrand*

Find out more about the books featured here at
www.business-minds.com